HAUNTED COLUMBIA, MISSOURI

HAUNTED COLUMBIA, MISSOURI

Mary Collins Barile

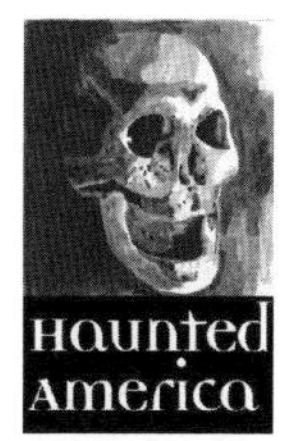

Published by Haunted America
A Division of The History Press
Charleston, SC
www.historypress.net

Front cover: Photograph courtesy of the author.
Back cover: Photograph by Tina Edholm. Insert courtesy of the author.
All images are from the author's collection unless otherwise noted.

First published 2016

Manufactured in the United States

ISBN 978.1.46713.618.1

Library of Congress Control Number: 2016936014

CONTENTS

Contents

ACKNOWLEDGEMENTS

There are many people who contributed personal stories and photographs to this collection, and for their generosity and time, I am grateful. Some asked that I not mention their names or specific locations of certain events, but know that each of these stories has been shared in detail, and I have little doubt the experiences were as real to the teller as I hope they will be to readers. In addition, thank you to those friends who followed me through cemeteries, over dark hills and into haunted houses and offered advice and information. They include Sarah Arrandale, Mary Arrandale, Linda Cooperstock, Tina Edholm, James Henderson, Arlene Hoose and Jane Lago. Ben Gibson and Rick Delaney are the best editors a writer could ask for, and Arcadia/The History Press is always a delight to work with. Tina Edholm's photographs capture the mystery of hauntings with beauty and style. Finally, to the staff of the Missouri Humanities Council, your support has been most appreciated.

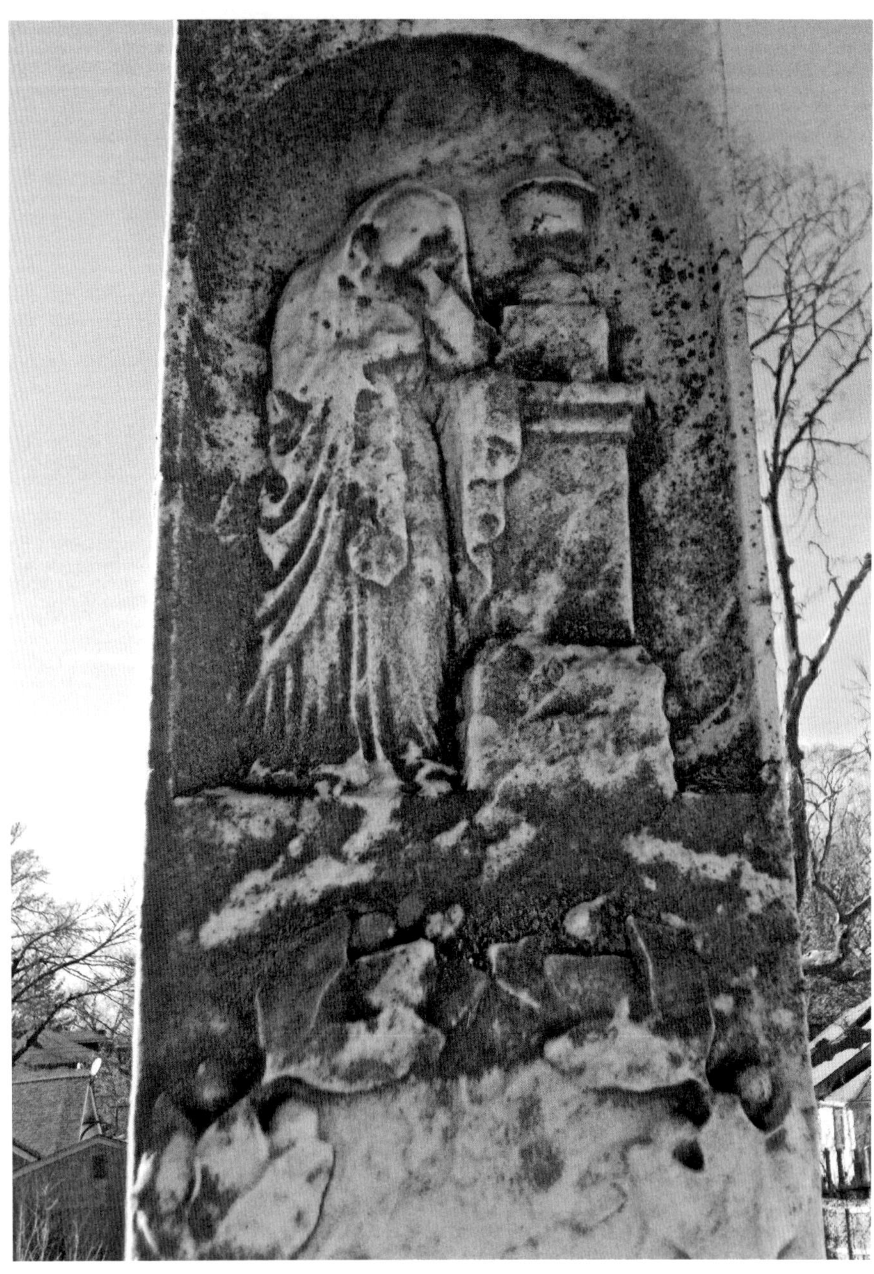

Grave markers often included depictions of mourning women leaning against the memorial of the departed.

A Note on the Text

I use "spirits" and "ghosts" interchangeably, and while some experts in the world of hauntings may disagree, I shall continue to do so until taken to task by an emissary from beyond the veil.

Readers of *The Haunted Boonslick* may be familiar with a few of the stories shared here. Since Columbia, Missouri, was within the Boonslick region, duplication was unavoidable, but I hope there are enough additions to make up for this lapse.

INTRODUCTION

Ghosts have haunted Missouri's history for centuries, beginning with the Mississippian culture, slipping into lodges of the Osage, sitting atop the wagon trains of nineteenth-century emigrants, pushing Ouija boards to and fro and poking their ectoplasm into modern tales. Ghost stories were told on the trail and in schoolhouses, general stores and lonely cabins. It should be no surprise that the best description of a ghost story appeared in the *Autobiography of Mark Twain*:

> *I can feel again the creepy joy which quivered through me when the time for the ghost story was reached—I can remember the howling of the wind and the quaking of the house on stormy nights. . . . I can remember how very dark that room was, in the dark of the moon, and how packed it was with ghostly stillness when one woke up by accident away in the night . . . and how dismal was the hoo-hooing of the owl and the wailing of the wolf, sent mourning by on the night wind.*

A ghost story does more than entertain storyteller and listener: it is the only way to experience death and return to the living world. The Missouri ghost canon includes murder, revenge, loss, retribution, suicide and tomfoolery in stories about white ladies, vanishing hitchhikers, unburied bodies, untethered souls and mysterious lights and sounds. Settlers brought along their tales from the Celtic and Germanic cultures, rife with appalling apparitions and traditions for summoning or dealing with the dead. Their ghosts still flicker among graveyards and along roadsides, frightening the weary traveler while answering no questions about the next life.

Ghosts appear to extract revenge, as with the black carriage of Overton, which haunts the back roads and holds the living to promises made to the dead. Or they seek companionship, as did the hermit spook of Clark's Fork, which appeared annually at local farms. Sometimes, they warn, as did a grave robber's mother who saved her son from being lynched. Some ghosts appear to protect, others to relive their past and some to just terrify. At a Missouri picnic, two men got into a knife fight, with one cutting off the other's head. But instead of falling over, the dead man was guided by his talking head to replace it atop his neck and then ran off into the night. Ghost stories served as entertainment, community bonding and more practical uses, as noted by Douglass Stewart in an essay, "Memories of Old Spring Hill," from Livingston County:

> *I remember that when a child, one* [story] *telling of seeing apparitions and balls of fire flying up and down the hollows on each side of the town. It was told of Dr. George Williams, a physician, and resident, that on many occasions while returning from nightly visits, a ghost would jump up and ride home with him on his horse. Some of the town women told of seeing "things" while attending the sick bed. I recall my father telling of meeting Bob Bray one evening just after dusk. He had just met a man with no head, wheeling off John Simpson's wheelbarrow. Another story was that Willis Griffin, who was clerking for John Dolfs* [a shop owner] *and sleeping in the store room, was awakened by a noise and on getting up, found a spook behind the counter measuring off the goods and when he spoke to it, it disappeared through the wall. Many, many such other stories were told. Of course, they all had a tendency to keep the children frightened so they stayed in at night.*

(Ghosts and haunting traditions were part of African traditional beliefs, but these were usually transcribed by white viewers and treated as evidence of witchcraft and sorcery. The definitive study of ghost stories told by black slaves in the United States remains to be undertaken.)

The grab bag of Missouri ghost stories expanded when spiritualism was founded in 1848, and sisters Kate, Margaret and Leah Fox sparked interest in "the other side." Missourians flocked to séances to interact with mediums and talk with the dead through rapping and automatic writing.

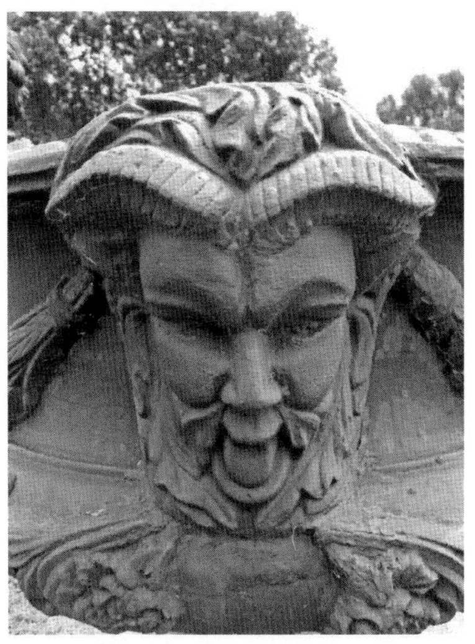

This sculpture was part of a fountain and urn. In the nineteenth century, cemeteries were often designed like parks, offering families a peaceful place to visit with the dead.

In a world where death could arrive early and swiftly, when cholera traveled with the steamboats and a woman could be fine at breakfast and dead by evening, the solace found in talking with those who passed was enormous. Enemies of spiritualism, including the Reverend A.T. Osborn, gave lectures on hypnotism throughout the state, debunking table rapping and revealing the tricks of mediums. But loss and grief drove people to reach beyond the veil. The talking board, also called the Ouija board, received its patent in 1890 and gained prominence because of the ease with which a user could communicate with spirits. By 1897, the *Kansas City Journal* was advertising the boards as marvelous Christmas gifts, since it was much faster to point to a letter than rap it out. Mark Twain understood that and wrote about spirit rappings in the *Territorial Enterprise* of January 1866:

> *I had a very dear friend, who, I had heard, had gone to the spirit land, or perdition, or some of those places, and I desired to know something concerning him. There was something so awful, though, about talking with living, sinful lips to the ghostly dead, that I could hardly bring myself to rise and speak. But at last I got tremblingly up and said with low and reverent voice: "Is the spirit of John Smith present?"*
>
> *Whack! whack! whack!*
>
> *God bless me. I believe all the dead and damned John Smiths between hell and San Francisco tackled that poor little table at once! I was considerably set back— stunned, I may say. The audience urged me to go on, however, and I said:*
>
> *What did you die of?*
>
> *The Smiths answered to every disease and casualty that man can die of.*
>
> *Where did you die!*
>
> *They answered yes to every locality I could name while my geography held out.*

Are you happy where you are?
There was a vigorous and unanimous "No!" from the late Smiths.
Is it warm there?
An educated Smith seized the medium's hand and wrote:
It's no name for it.

True to the rough pioneer "spirits," some ghost stories developed from practical jokes played on nervous farmers. At least one story is told of a ghost that consisted of lathing and sheets and was pulled out of a well by ropes and pulley to terrify passersby. Another, from 1842, comes from Kirksville's *Salt River Journal*, whose editor noted that this was already an old story in Missouri. A man stops at a tavern and is told that the only room left is haunted and that inhabitants hear a voice asking, "Do . . . you . . . want . . . to . . . be . . . shaved?" The man takes the room, searches it and goes to bed, only to wake and hear a faint whisper that sounds like the ghost. He bravely gets out of bed and searches the room to discover that the wind causes tree limbs to rub together and that an imaginative man would hear, "Do you want to be shaved?" He tries to sleep but is kept awake by the loud and drunken gamblers in the next room. So he gets up, puts on a sheet and bursts into the next room, calling, "Do you want to be shaved?" The terrified gamblers run out, the man takes a large amount of money left on the table and goes back to his room. The next morning, the now sober gamblers are telling about the ghost's visit and their stolen money. The guest smiles to himself, has breakfast and leaves, "many hundred dollars richer by the adventure."

Newspaper articles of the nineteenth century point to a robust Missouri belief in ghosts and spiritualism. Stories of haunted houses across the United States were reprinted in Missouri newspapers, including one of a sheriff who let out that his jail was haunted, resulting in a reduction in crime, as potential scofflaws did not want to spend the night alone in the cells. From the headless dog and white woman who appeared around Cape Girardeau on the Bend Road to the Chariton County ghost rider who galloped alongside wagons at night before disappearing into thin air, ghosts abounded. In Chariton County, the Goben Hotel was known for an apparition that would appear and sit by the inhabitants, then disappear when spoken to. Two families eventually abandoned the building after the ghostly appearances continued. But no matter how much fun could be had at the expense of an unsuspecting victim, no matter how brave or pragmatic a settler, no matter how squeaky a board or noisy a squirrel, the reason folks jumped at ghost stories is because they believed in them.

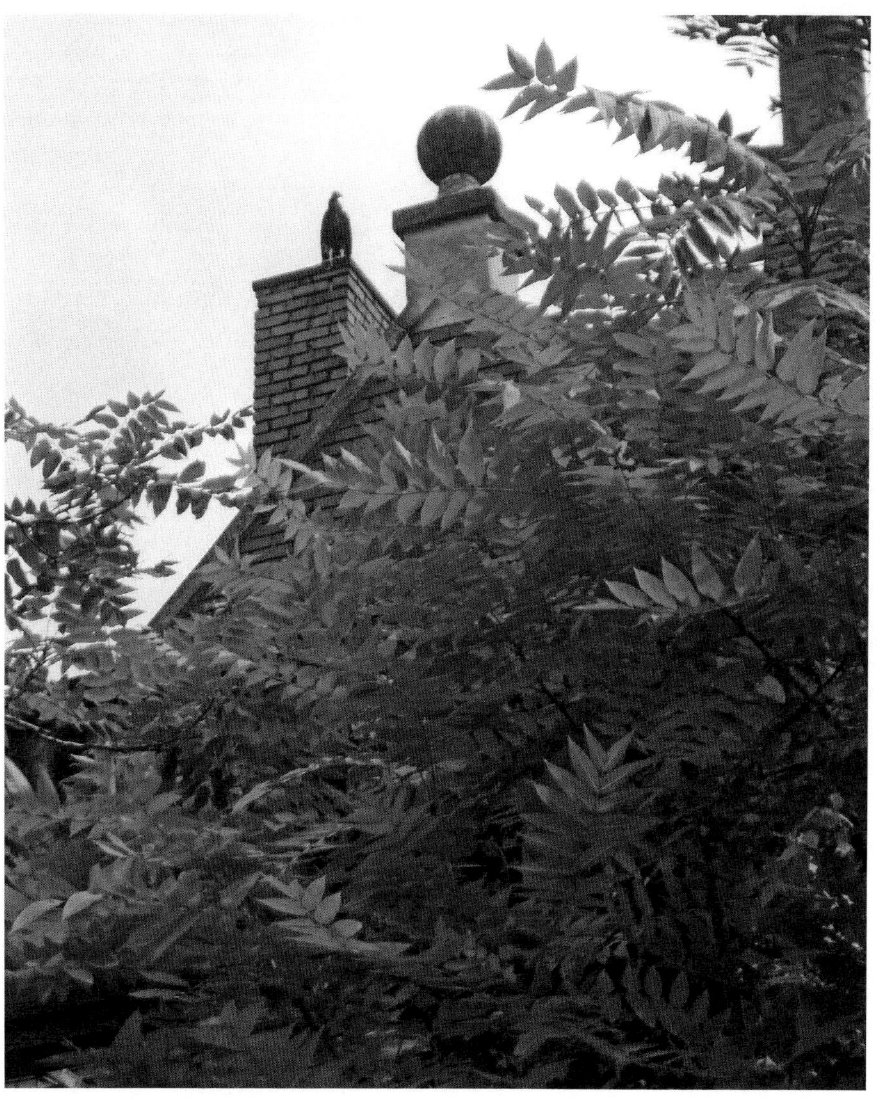

A buzzard stops by this cemetery.

What exactly is it about Missouri that attracts hauntings? Some scholars insist that ghosts appear because of the landscape: with its deep ravines and rolling prairies, Missouri offers a stage easily set to entertain both ghost and visitor for a night. The Missouri and Mississippi Rivers throw off fogs and mists that baffled even Mark Twain, who wrote about a haunted steamboat caught in the throes of a cursed current. Another of his tales had a ghost pilot as a guardian angel. Investigators swear that water and limestone act as catalysts and magnifying lenses for ghosts, and Missouri is built on both. Then again, who has not felt the power of a prairie crossroads at midnight, when lost in the country and seeking a safe haven of light and companionship? If the landscape is not enough to invite ghosts, perhaps no figures are more strongly associated with Missouri in the public's mind than the James brothers, Frank and Jesse, who were born and raised in the state to raise hell in the world. Even they are associated with a ghost story, reprinted here for perhaps the first time from the *Butler Weekly Times* (August 29, 1888):

> *Jesse James and the Phantom Horseman*
>
> *The story of the phantom horseman was always firmly believed by the companions of Frank and Jesse James. Frank was always the least superstitious of the men who rode with the celebrated raiders. Jesse, however, had a strong vein of superstition in his composition and firmly believed that the phantom horseman was his own peculiar banshee. He frequently asserted that the appearance of the apparition was intended as a warning or foreboded evil. The first time Frank James saw the apparition was one night when he, Jesse, and several other members of the outlawed nightriders were riding. . . . As they emerged from the heavy shadows of the trees, where the two roads met, they came upon an open space where the moon shone brightly on the converging cross roads.*
>
> *There, distinctly outlined in the bright moonlight, sat a man on a coal black horse. The moon shone brightly on the polished trappings of the steed. Horse and rider remained motionless as if silently challenging the right of the party to the way. Jesse drew his revolver to fire, but was stopped by the exclamation of one of the party, who exclaimed: "My God, it is a ghost!" The figure remained motionless and seemed to gradually fade away before their eyes as Jesse turned his horse and took the other road. "I've seen him before," said Jesse, but refused to offer any further explanation. It is said that several other members of the so-called James gang have seen the phantom, among them Bill Ryan and Dick Little, and can vouch for the authenticity of this account. The phantom was generally alluded to as "Jesse's ghost," and is said to have appeared to him shortly before his death* [1882]. *Jesse seemed to recognize the phantom as the ghost of somebody he had known in life, but was strangely silent on the question and never vouchsafed any explanation.*

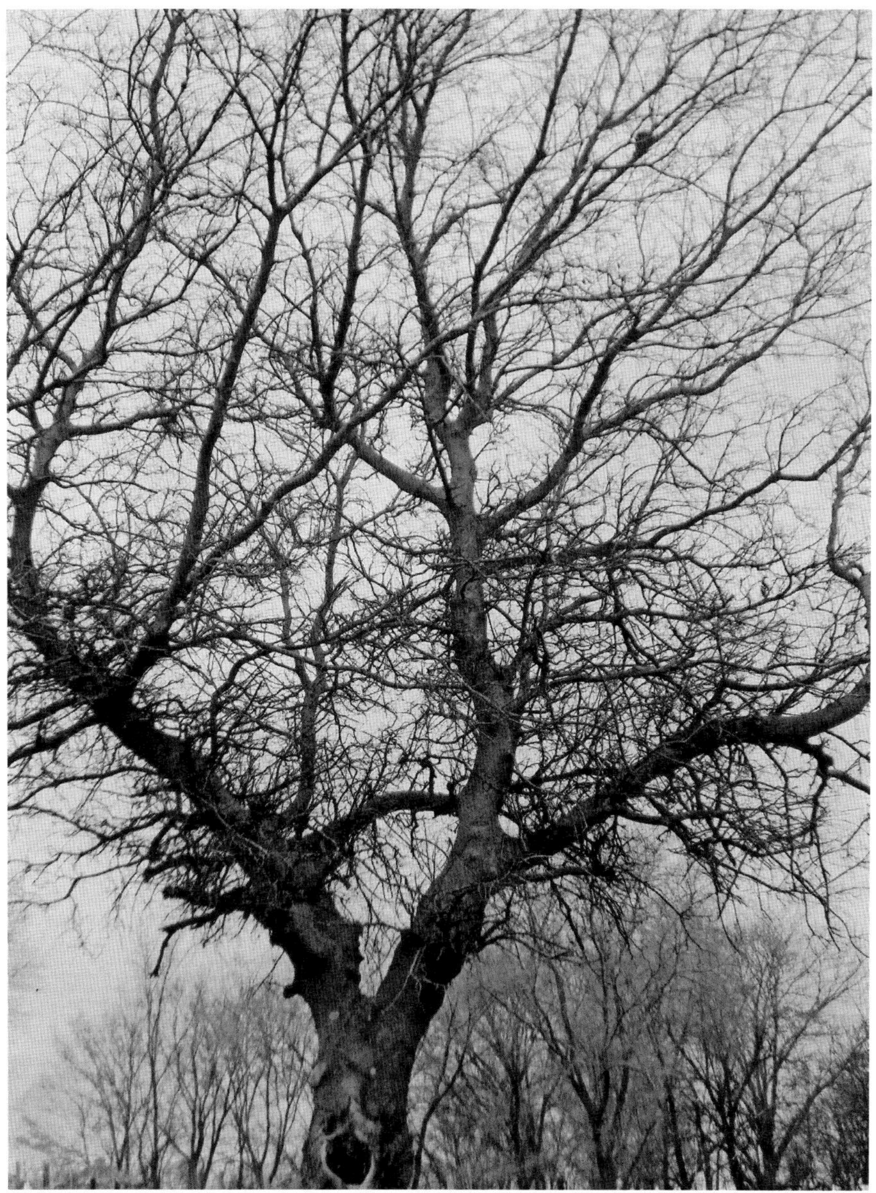

Some ghost stories arose because travelers mistook trees for figures and scraping branches for creaking horrors.

Newspapers offered a glimpse into the ghost world of nineteenth-century Missouri. One humorous "story" in the 1887 *Butler Weekly Times* told of a benighted man who was haunted day and night by a picture of a pointing finger, until he realized it was guiding him to an excellent sale at the local store. The *Richmond Democrat* carried a story advising people that ghosts wanted to share information or get something off their minds. (The article also noted that it was notoriously difficult to sell a haunted house.) Other articles, like one from the *Marble Hill Press* in 1896, reported on "real" hauntings, such as the one in South Dakota, "where witnesses over several nights heard music, saw full body apparitions wander through the rooms." There was the phantom horseman along the Missouri River near the Dakotas who was reported in a letter to a St. Louis newspaper and reprinted in the *Mexico Weekly Ledger* in 1887. In the story, a military officer noted that one night, as he was heading back to the fort in a wagon, he saw a horseman following after him. Calling to the shadowy figure, the officer received no answer; when he stopped and turned, he could see the horseman galloping after him but coming no closer. The officer spurred his horse to a gallop and headed for a bridge, which he crossed safely, but not before hearing what sounded like "a thousand horses galloping down

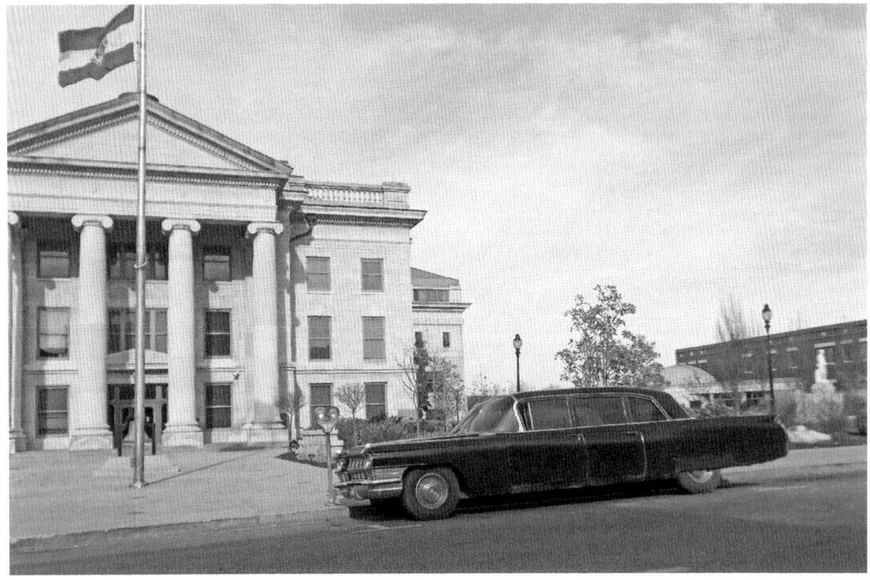

The Columbia courthouse stands along Broadway, the city's main road for nearly two centuries.

a wooden pavement." On another occasion, Alexander McKinzie met the same phantom, but this time the ghost was galloping in the opposite direction and passed McKinzie in a rush of sound; as the region's sheriff, McKinzie was considered a sober and trustworthy man. So, whether or not the stories were set in Missouri, Missourians heard about hauntings and knew they were not alone when it came to ghosts.

Columbia's own ghost stories began centuries ago, with indigenous groups who believed that spirits could return and haunt them, even as shamans traveled to the spirit world seeking wisdom and help. Ghost stories were recorded early in the settlement period in newspapers and gazetteers, but the golden age of terror really blossomed in the mid-nineteenth century. Unlike formal literature, ghost stories are born in the telling, and keeping them alive requires active communication, sharing and repetition. Fortunately, Columbia provided all of that in the form of college campuses, where stories were cultivated and perfected over generations. It is a measure of the strength of legends and tales that old and new coexist comfortably, adapting to the community's need for continuity and companionship. Ghost stories can also reassure even as they scare: there is no need to be frightened of something that you can ultimately control if you know the rules and techniques for dealing with ghosts. This book contains Columbia stories that have been polished over generations, reflecting back to us our fears and memories. Whether or not you believe in ghosts, you will find in these stories an unknown Columbia. But be careful: it's a place best explored in the light of day.

Columbia's History

Members of the Mississippian culture settled in the Columbia region as early as AD 1400, but little is known of their life in the region, and less is known of their lore and traditions. It is possible that French and Spanish explorers and trappers made their way into mid-Missouri as early as the seventeenth century, but it wasn't until the Louisiana Purchase that a U.S. government survey was undertaken. In 1803, Lewis and Clark traversed this region on their way west, impressed by the prairies, bluffs and wildlife along the Missouri River. Migration to the Boonslick region, named after a natural salt lick worked by sons of the Boone family, increased during the War of 1812, when settlers moved into the area encompassed by modern Boone County. Although settlers arrived from New York, Vermont and Connecticut, migration from Virginia, Kentucky and Tennessee was so great that the area around present-day Columbia was eventually nicknamed Little Dixie. The region developed into a center of agriculture, with hemp, tobacco, wheat and corn shipped downriver to St. Louis. Columbia had its bureaucratic beginnings in 1818, when the Smithton Land Company purchased acreage and established Smithton, named in honor of General T.A. Smith, the receiver in the Franklin Land Office and an original investor in the town site. By 1819, the Smithton investors were advertising in the *Missouri Intelligencer* for someone to build a "double hewed log house, shingled roof and stone chimneys, one story and a half high.... They will also contract for digging and a well," an activity that proved prescient in the light of later problems. Boone County was eventually trimmed from Howard County and established in 1820; by 1821, Missouri was a state. But in a reversal of fortune, Smithton realized that its wells were not enough for a growing town. The lack of a dependable water source forced the Smithtonians to pack up the entire settlement and move it a mile away, near Hinkson Creek and the Flat Branch. The new village was named Columbia, in honor of the young country, and the city began its history.

The original plat for Columbia included more than four hundred lots, with land set aside for private and public use. Broadway was part of the Boonslick Trail, which ran from St. Louis to Franklin, where it connected with the eastern terminus of the Santa Fe Trail. By 1824, there were 160 people living in Columbia, and the population tripled again in a decade. The city was bustling, with businesses and homes lining streets that were uncommonly wide for the time. That was due to the vision of William Jewell, who insisted on streets that were big enough to host livestock sales without impeding human travelers. (He also supported regulations to reduce the dumping of offal from slaughterhouses and increase the number of gutters, drains and sidewalks.) By 1837, the *Gazetteer of Missouri* noted that Columbia had twelve stores, three churches, a mail route and a university—a far cry from the first ramshackle cabins and dry well.

Part of Columbia's success was due to the establishment of private and public schools. In 1833, Lucy Wales established the Columbia Female

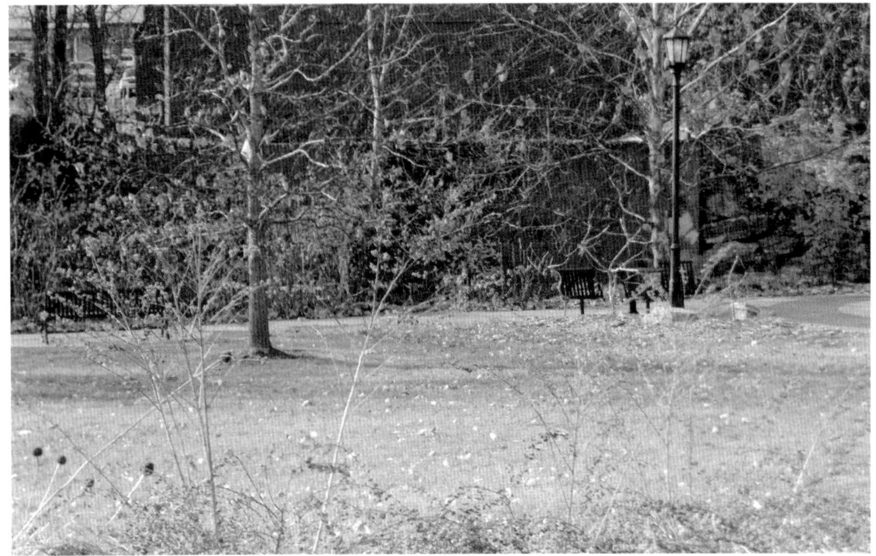

This small park along the Flat Branch marks part of Smithton.

Academy, which later evolved into Stephens College. A few years later, the town leaders decided to compete for the first state university established within the old Louisiana Territory. More than 900 townspeople pledged $118,000 in support of the idea, beating out Boonville and other towns in the process. In 1839, the University of Missouri opened in Columbia. The Christian Female College was founded next, in 1851, and was later known as Columbia College. By 1860, the *Missouri State Gazetteer and Business Directory* noted that Columbia was a thriving center of education and commerce with a population of more than 1,400 townsfolk. Among them were dressmakers, surgeons, wagon makers, tinsmiths, factory owners, cabinetmakers, newspaper editors, livery stables owners and milliners.

CIVIL WAR BLUES . . . AND GRAYS

Throughout the Columbia area, plantations grew from small farms in the mid-nineteenth century, and slavery was the engine that kept the growth moving; there were more than five thousand slaves listed in the 1860 U.S. Census for Boone County, 25 percent of the population. The Civil War twisted Missouri into knots, and Columbia struggled to maintain its equilibrium, a pro-Union city yet home to many slaveholders. Newspapers ran announcements of meetings in celebration of both Confederate and Union victories, and families were split apart. Federal troops occupied the University of Missouri's grounds in 1861, living in the school's buildings and using University Hall as a military prison. Despite arrests, incarcerations and prisoner trades, at least one story had a happy ending: more than a dozen Confederate troops escaped when a prisoner's mother smuggled a knife and saw into the prison using a baked turkey as cover. The men cut a hole in the floor and fled to Rocheport and safety.

Like residents of most Missouri towns, citizens of Columbia were fearful of bushwhacker raids, so they organized the Columbia Tiger Company, a civilian group that dug a ditch around the courthouse and patrolled around the building's dome, using spyglasses to watch for attacks. The Tigers also set up a blockhouse on Eighth Street and Broadway, and in the event bushwhackers were sighted, bells were rung and additional troops called in, activities that convinced the attackers there might be easier pickings elsewhere in the county. Despite all the preparations, a battle took place along Eighth and Ninth Streets south of Broadway, when Confederate soldiers escaped

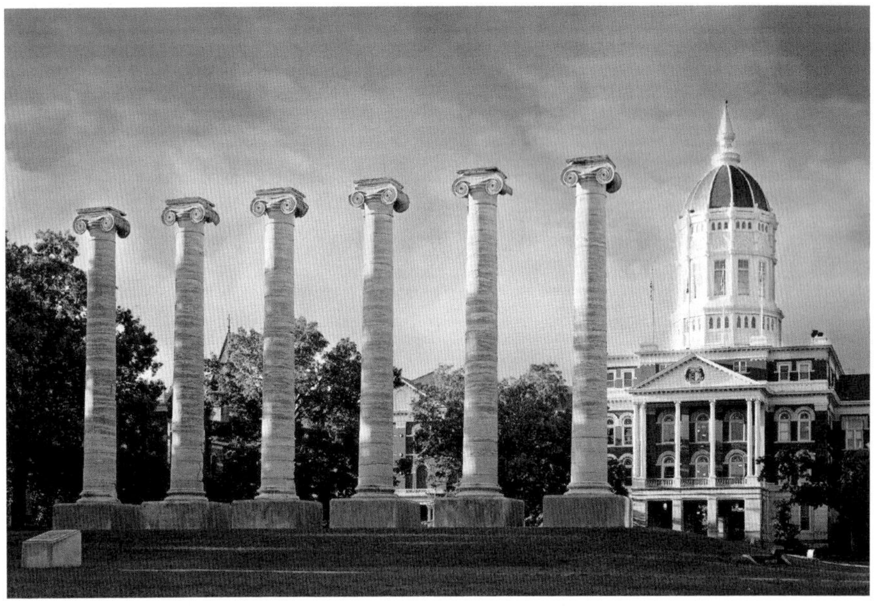

The University of Missouri Columns (with Jesse Hall in the background.) The Columns are all that remain of the original Academic Hall, which burned to the ground. *Photograph by Tina Edholm.*

with Federal horses. The Union general believed Columbians had alerted the Southern troops about the lack of guards; in retaliation, he planned to burn down Columbia and the university. Robert L. Todd (cousin of Mary Todd Lincoln) told him that the battle was the general's fault, since he had no business being at a ceremony instead of directing his troops. Todd, who was the first graduate of the University of Missouri, thundered at the officer, "If you set fire to and burn our town and our university, the friends of our town and our university will kindle a fire under you, and I tremble for you at the result." Although the town was saved, the Federal troops did damage to university buildings. North Todd Gentry noted in "Some Incidents of the Civil War in Columbia and Boone County" that Congress eventually provided $5,000 in reparation, which was used to erect the university's South Eighth Street entrance.

Columbia repaired, regrouped and regrew after the war, adding improved sewage, water and lighting systems; welcoming the automobile, movies and telephones; and soon looking forward to the new century. But as with many cities of the time, Columbia was essentially two places: Columbia and Sharp End, a thriving black community along the Flat Branch Creek. Sharp End had its own newspaper, the *Professional World*; a number of churches and small businesses; and the music and financial investments of musician John William "Blind" Boone and his manager/brother-in-law, John Lange Jr. Both men contributed improvements to the black and white communities that are still seen today.

As Columbia heads toward its bicentennial, the face of downtown is undergoing another change, with student housing, new commercial ventures and university expansion. Today, the population is more than 117,000, and the city thrives. But with all this change comes disruption, and with disruption, according to old lore, come ghosts.

DEAD AND DYING AND GONE AND BACK

This is a book about ghosts and ghost stories, but where do they come from and why? Perhaps it makes sense to understand a bit more about a ghost's journey to ghosthood before the stories begin.

Until World War II, many people prepared bodies at home for burial, so the intimacy of death was part of daily life. Missouri's death and burial practices reflected the many different cultures that shared a region ruled at various times by Spanish, French and Americans. Throughout the state are graves that reflect diverse traditions. Burials began with Native American observances, including possible mound interments that are still to be seen along the Missouri River bluffs. Among European settlers, the oldest emigrant cemetery in Missouri is St. Genevieve's, where people have been buried since 1787. There was quite a difference between a graveyard and a cemetery. Graveyards surrounded churches and were owned and maintained by the church and congregation, so the burials could be carefully regulated—whites here, slaves there, unbaptized children beyond that marker, suicides over there and so on. On the other hand, cemeteries (from the Greek word for "dormitory" or "sleeping place") were owned by organizations and did not have to be associated with a church.

In early Missouri days, graveyards were often haphazardly arranged and cared for, growing as the congregation expanded without plan or process. Events such as cholera epidemics could result in more bodies than burial space, resulting in the exhumation of older burials or the reopening of previously used graves. Few people were comfortable around a graveyard, no matter how picturesque, since sanitary practices were challenged by weather, geology and the inclination of grave diggers. The older the graveyard, the more inclined it was to be a place best avoided after dark. Mark Twain recalled the old Hannibal graveyard that played such an important role in *The Adventures of Tom Sawyer*:

> *It was a graveyard of the old-fashioned Western kind. It was on a hill, about a mile and a half from the village. It had a crazy board fence around it, which leaned inward in places, and outward the rest of the time, but stood upright nowhere. Grass and weeds grew rank over the whole cemetery. All the old graves were sunken in, there was not a tombstone on the place; round-topped, worm-eaten boards staggered over the graves, leaning for support and finding none. "Sacred to the memory of" So-and-So had been painted on them once, but it could no longer have been read on the most of them now, even if there had been light.*

This must have made a strong impression on Twain, for in a story from 1870, he returned to the theme of uncared-for cemeteries, using a skeleton as narrator in "The Curious Dream":

> *Yes, sir, thirty years ago I laid me down there, and was happy. . . . Everything was pleasant. I was in a good neighborhood, for all the dead people that lived near me belonged to the best families in the city. Our posterity appeared to think the world of us. They kept our graves in the very best condition; the fences were always in faultless repair, head-boards were kept painted or whitewashed, and were replaced with new ones as soon as they began to look rusty or decayed; monuments were kept upright, railings intact and bright, the rose-bushes and shrubbery trimmed, trained, and free from blemish, the walks clean and smooth and graveled. But that day is gone by. . . .* [Now] *bless you, there isn't a grave in our cemetery that doesn't leak, not one. Every time it rains in the night we have to climb out and roost in the trees and sometimes we are wakened suddenly by the chilly water trickling down the back of our necks . . . with our joints rattling drearily and the wind wheezing through our ribs! Many a time we have perched there . . . then come down, stiff and chilled through and drowsy, and borrowed each other's skulls to bail out our graves with.*

That the burial ground played an important role in local culture was echoed by a Missouri editor in the *Democratic Banner*, who noted on August 31, 1846:

> *There is nothing in our opinion, which speaks more favorably of the moral feeling of a community than a proper respect for the memory of departed friends. Show us a village grave yard which gives daily evidence of the care and attention of the citizens around to the memory of those who were near and dear to them in this world, and we will show you a people remarkable for their industry, sobriety and goodness of heart. But on the other hand, show us a neglected graveyard whose dilapidated walls afford no barrier to the beasts of the field, which roam over and burrow in it, and we will show you an immoral and vicious community.*

On this same note, the *Sedalia Weekly Bazoo* (1890) described "A Haunted Cemetery—Neglected Graves and Broken Tombstones Tell the Story of the Heartless Desertion—The sickening odors which issue from a trench filled with those who died of small-pox—Queer kinds of ghosts which stalk about at night and in broad daylight—A headless white horse that gallops over graves—Sudden disappearance of a wagon!"

After these spectacular headlines, the reporter describes visiting the graveyard, noting that moles had dug into trenches where more than fifty

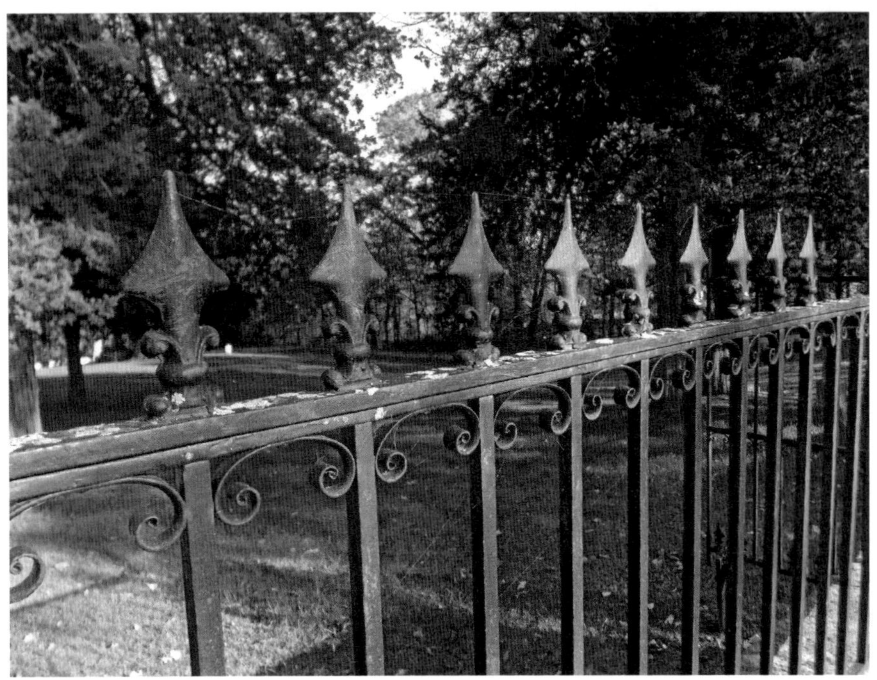

Some cemeteries were decorated with elaborate fences, walks and seating.

smallpox victims were buried in the early days (and he imagines the smell). Formerly a Negro burying ground, it "is now property of the White estate." Local families said that ghosts roamed the cemetery day and night, and one man, a grave digger during the smallpox epidemic "eighteen years ago" (1872), described seeing a man holding a lantern and leading a horse and wagon. Then, slowly, each of the figures disappeared: man, horse and, finally, the wagon. The witness explained that he found wagon tracks where the ghosts had been but that the tracks just stopped. Other people reported seeing a rider on a headless white horse, with vivid descriptions of hearing the saddle squeaking and watching as the horse disappeared into the air.

Cemeteries had architecture and layouts specific to a community's needs. There were curved drives around small lakes and rows of cedars that made the sites feel like a park, offering visitors a chance to stroll and visit graves of friends and family. The Columbia Cemetery (located on Broadway) was established in 1820 as a common burying ground where anyone might purchase a plot in the main section—as long as he was white and Christian. Families and friends attended funerals whenever possible, but distance and weather could make that impossible in the winter. These problems were solved by providing a receiving vault, used to store coffins until interment was possible. Columbia Cemetery has one of only two vaults of this type in the state.

According to the *Columbia Evening Missourian* in 1922, burials in the Columbia Cemetery were conveyed there by pallbearers: "It was the custom for men to carry large silk bandana pocket handkerchiefs. Three of these were placed under the coffin, the ends held by six men, and in this way the body was born[e] to its last resting place." Receiving vaults were promoted as a way to avoid a nineteenth-century terror: premature burial. Even with modern medical skills, calling time of death is a difficult procedure. Although the number of premature burials was probably lower than Edgar Allan Poe would have one believe, the possibility—and the fear—was real. Official steps were taken in Missouri to avoid any mistakes, from issuing death certificates (an official might recognize flickering signs of life) to building vaults where bodies were stored until "signs of decay" were evident and death was assured. One of the few Missouri stories about premature burial took place in Rocheport and was recorded in the 1882 *History of Boone County*:

> *In 1849 cholera again visited Rocheport. Several cases occurred. Alexander Graver* [sometimes listed as O'Connell], *driver of the stage from*

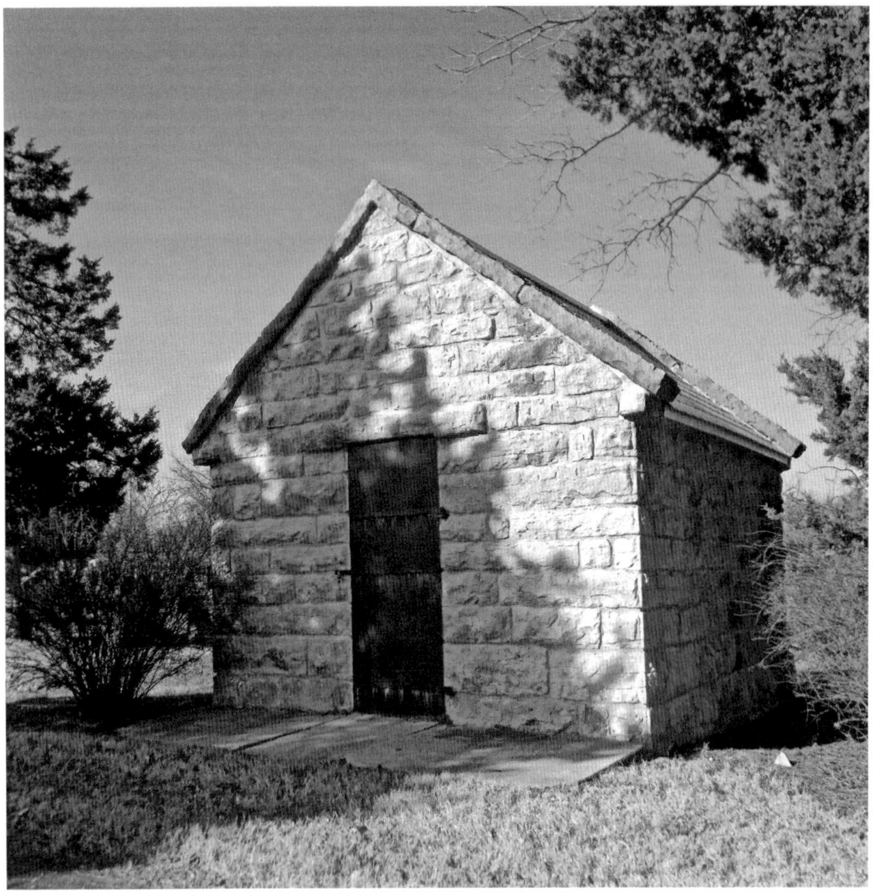

The receiving vault at the Columbia Cemetery, one of only two remaining in the state.

> *Rocheport to Columbia, came close to being buried alive. He was attacked with cholera and to all appearances died. His coffin had been prepared and full preparations made for his burial, when a Dr. Buster discovered signs of life, and by dint of fresh blisters, vigorous rubbing, etc. restored the alleged "corpse" to full animation.*

Cholera was among the deadliest diseases to sweep across Missouri, and the 1849 epidemic was especially severe, carrying off thousands of victims. The disease was spread by contaminated water; a victim could be fine in the morning and dead by afternoon through enormous loss of fluids. If a disease can be considered intelligent, then cholera was among the most learned killers, as it found the perfect way to move from city to city: carried along by the steamboats plying the Mississippi and Missouri Rivers.

By the mid-nineteenth century, Missouri cemeteries provided opportunities for another, more human plague: resurrectionists (body snatchers), who "acquired" new bodies for medical students. One in particular had a connection with Columbia. Joseph McDowell, born on April 1, 1805, in Kentucky, received a medical degree from Transylvania University. He became a leading anatomist and teacher and, in 1840, founded the medical department of Kemper College (St. Louis), later known as the Missouri Medical College or McDowell's Medical College. The school was associated for a short time with the University of Missouri. At that time, medical students could graduate without having touched a cadaver, and McDowell was intent on changing that. But cadavers were difficult to come by. Missouri law allowed unclaimed bodies to be sent to medical schools, but the "distribution system" could not provide enough for class needs. The other option was grave-robbing, detested by the public but considered sensible by desperate doctors. Cemetery employees were often bribed to weigh down coffins with rocks and bring the bodies to doctors.

Other times, teacher and students would exhume a body for study. McDowell once acquired a body and was in the dissecting room when a crowd broke into the college intent on lynching him. McDowell quickly hid the body but soon realized he was trapped by the mob. According to a story he told, the ghost of his mother appeared and motioned him to one of the dissecting tables. He climbed onto one and covered himself with a sheet not a second too soon, as the crowd surged in. Wary of the dead, the mob only glanced at the covered "corpses" before leaving. McDowell said he thanked his mother's spirit for her quick thinking: saved by a ghost.

Families resorted to different innovations and protective measures to guard against the McDowells of the world. Missouri papers carried articles about ghouls and grave robbers, noting that a steel casket was a relatively inexpensive investment for peace of mind. As late as 1903, the *Professional World* (Columbia) carried a story about a Macon man who was interred in a "heavily constructed steel case with a patent lock." Other graves had a mortsafe, an iron cage that fit over the plot. (The Sappington Cemetery near Arrow Rock has a grave that employed a simpler method: iron bands holding it closed.) The *Sedalia Weekly Bazoo* noted in March 1884 that, before a murderer's grave had been disturbed, a prominent Kansas City doctor and an "obscure country doctor" had arrived in Sedalia, consulted with some "hard looking characters" and then left the city without registering at a hotel.

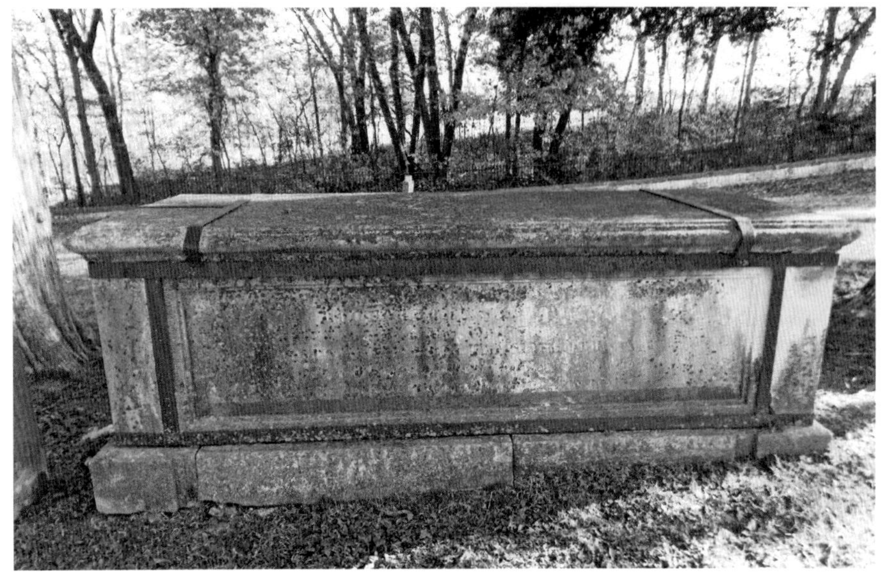

This aboveground sarcophagus was protected against intrusion by metal bands.

Later, a Mrs. Kelly received extensive coverage in the *Kansas City Journal* on October 31, 1898, when she discovered that her husband's body had been stolen. She had a premonition and insisted that the grave be opened, and more than two hundred people gathered to view the disinterment. The widow turned out to be right, and she "reeled and fell into the arms of her son," wept piteously and demanded that the ghouls be executed for the crime. "Just to think! The body of my poor, dead husband was buried only one week ago . . . his funeral cost me $183, and I paid $35 for a lot in the cemetery. The beautiful casket in which he was buried cost $83." The article noted that the Kansas City medical colleges received their bodies from the county farm and local hospitals and had no need of grave robbers to acquire subjects. The masterminds must have been from out of town.

WHICH WAY IS UP?

In Missouri, there are many different types of burial markers or coverings, and they often vary with the local traditions, the stonemason's skills and the date of death. A table tomb looks like its name: two supporting legs

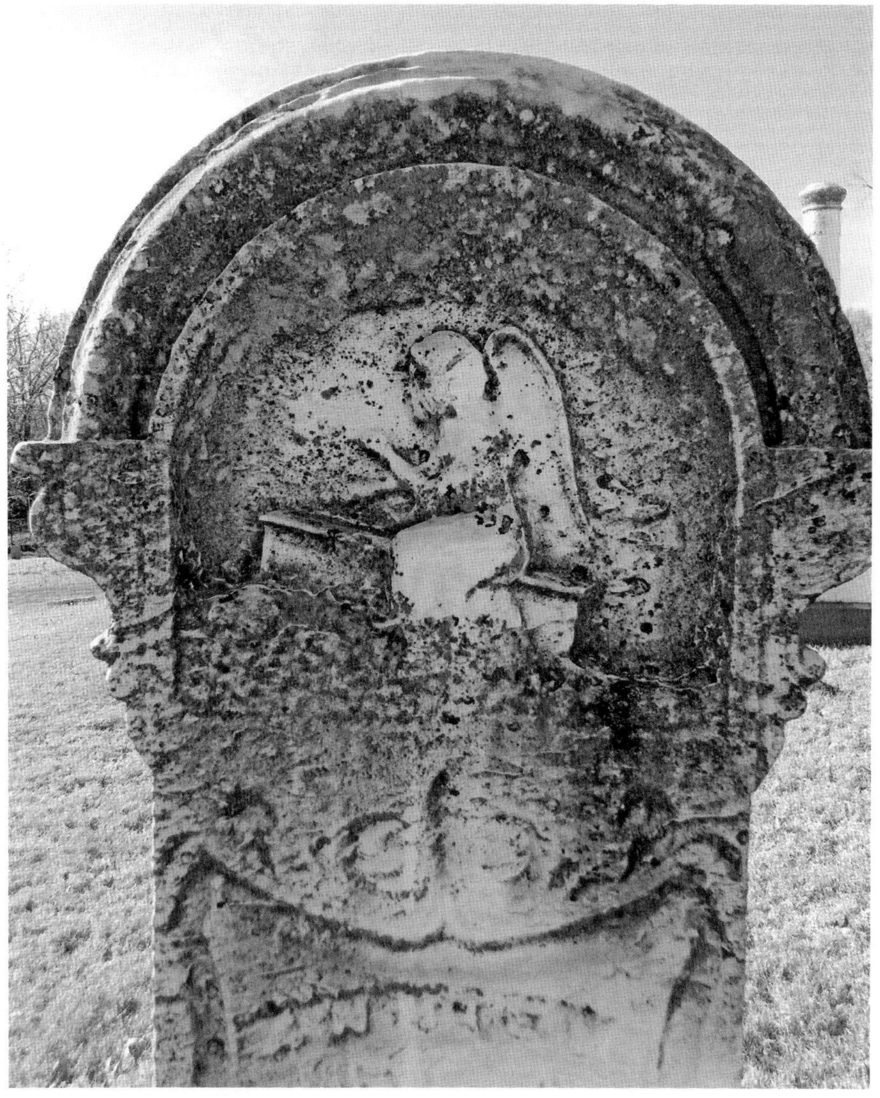

Sometimes the meaning of headstone carvings is a mystery. This appears to be an angel sitting on a floating casket and rowing.

or sides, with a flat, table surface. An oven tomb resembles a bake oven or shoebox covering the grave. Neither table nor oven tombs held bodies but were used to protect and mark the graves. Gravestones, headstones and tombstones are all objects used to mark graves. There were headstones (with names, date and quotations), footstones (with initials) and chest markers (flat pieces laid into the ground). The stones were carved with designs, symbols and quotations representing the deceased, their lives and deaths. Symbols had many layers of meanings, but among the most common—and obvious—were fingers pointing upward (to heaven) or downward (life cut short on earth), as well as angels, willows (sorrow), crosses, lilies, ivy (remembrance), broken chains (ended life), clasped hands (friendship or love) and lambs (children or infants). Other carvings are a bit more obscure; in the Columbia Cemetery, a stone is carved with an angel sitting atop a casket and rowing with an oar.

Cemeteries employed "tombstone censors" to ensure that epitaphs were tasteful. At least one Missouri censor had to nix the "shocking blasphemies" of atheists. The cenotaph, which resembles an obelisk, is not a gravestone; it is used as a memorial to someone whose body is not buried there. Graves were dug so a body faced the east—on Judgment Day, a person could sit up and look at the rising sun. A Missouri man, however, asked to be buried with his head to the south, since he believed he got his best rest when aligned with the earth's north and south electrical currents.

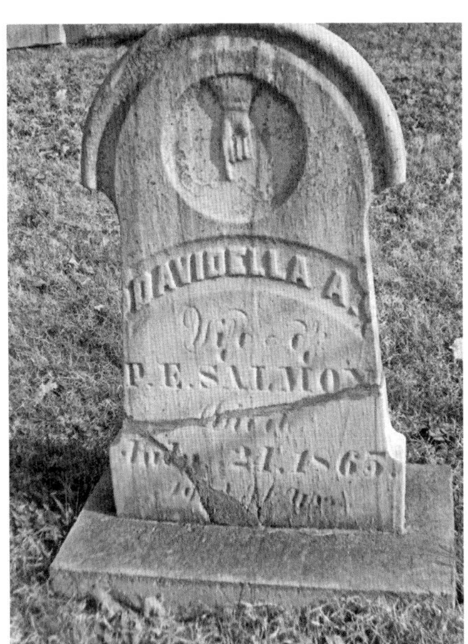

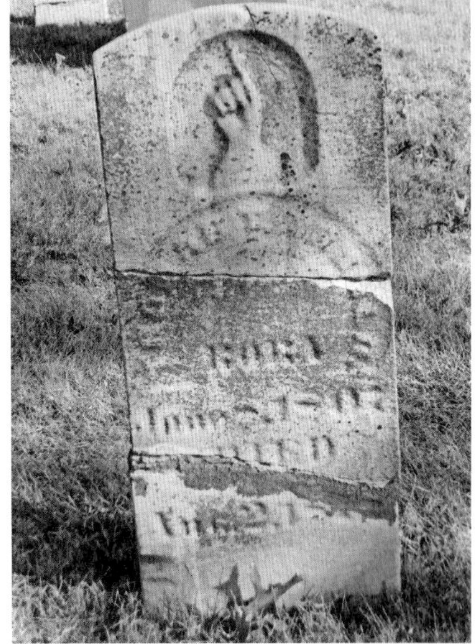

Left: The downward-pointing hand represented a life cut short, not a direction.

Right: The upward-pointing hand meant ascension to heaven.

The word "coffin" is ancient, having traveled from ancient Greek, to French and, finally, into English. The word originally meant a basket that held a body and, later, a boxlike container of wood or metal. Whatever its composition, a coffin always had a lid. And here is the ghoulish part: a coffin was shaped like the human body, which saved time, effort and wood during the building process. King Tut was buried in a coffin. On the other hand, a "casket" (from a French word for "box," particularly one that held jewelry or important items) is rectangular. These items went into the grave, a word from the German and Norse that at various times implied a cave or, less happily, scratching, scraping or digging. A sarcophagus (from the Greek for "flesh-eating stone") held either the body or the body, coffin and casket together and was usually displayed above the ground in a cemetery or inside a church. One Missouri coffin had a terrible ending. In 1890, the *Meriden Daily Republican* reported that a Sedalia woman died and her coffin was ordered from another town. By the time the coffin arrived, the body had begun to swell, so it was packed tightly in the box. The mourners were gathered for the services when, suddenly, decomposition caused the coffin to explode, blowing out the viewing window and allowing the deceased to stare out at the crowd. The story indicated that burial was immediate.

Native American Hauntings

The Native Americans who lived near Columbia had differing religious beliefs, depending on the tribe, but most shared the concept of the Manitou, a powerful spirit or creator force. White settlers recorded these traditions through place names like Big Moniteau Creek. (The Osage called the spirit *Wa-kon-da*.) Early explorers reported spirit paintings carved into stone and painted on rock faces, perhaps depicting a supernatural being invoked as protection for the land and its people. A rising moon, a star and a Manitou (or perhaps a shaman figure) were found on the bluffs near Rocheport, Missouri. Among the most spectacular of the paintings were those found near Alton, Illinois, high above the Mississippi River. Father Jacques Marquette, missionary and explorer, wrote of his first impression in the seventeenth century:

> *As we coasted along rocks frightful for their height and length, we saw two monsters painted on one of these rocks, which startled us at first, and on which the boldest Indian dare not gaze long. They are as large as a calf, with horns on the head like a deer, a fearful look, red eyes, bearded like a tiger, the face somewhat like a man's, the body covered with scales, and the tail so long that it twice makes the turn of the body, passing over the head and down between the legs, and ending at last in a fish's tail. Green, red, and a kind of black, are the colors employed.*

The depicted creature was called the "piasa." While some historians believe the word is from *paillisa*, French for "river bluffs," others say it is an old word for spirit creature. But it took the American talent for bunkum to change a religious belief into a monster. During the 1830s and '40s, a writer named John Russell, who specialized in rip-roaring adventure stories with a twisted version of the truth, wrote a magazine article purporting to tell the story of a giant Mississippi River bird that snatched people and flew away to its bluff-top nest. Russell's monster was a conflation of native beliefs, fossil hunting and great American hype. He created stories about the piasa that are still passed around as truth.

But other Native American stories have very long and old roots. Religious beliefs varied widely, but Native Americans who lived in the Missouri area had strong connections with the spirit world. The Omaha and related tribes called the Milky Way a path to eternity, where life continued but without sadness and struggle. When someone died, the camp kept bonfires and torches burning over four evenings, providing the spirit with light to see its way to the next world. After death, the souls who deserved peace were given a short path, while those who deserved punishment were sent to a long, wavy path, where they traveled for a long time and accounted for their life's behavior. The Omaha believed in ghosts that stayed near the living. Slain warriors were said to return to the battlefields, and their voices are heard in thunder, while ghost camps sometimes appeared and joined the living, where they were welcome for however long they stayed. However, the ghost that produced great fear was that of a murdered man who returned to camp for revenge. Some tribes buried the body of a murdered person facedown

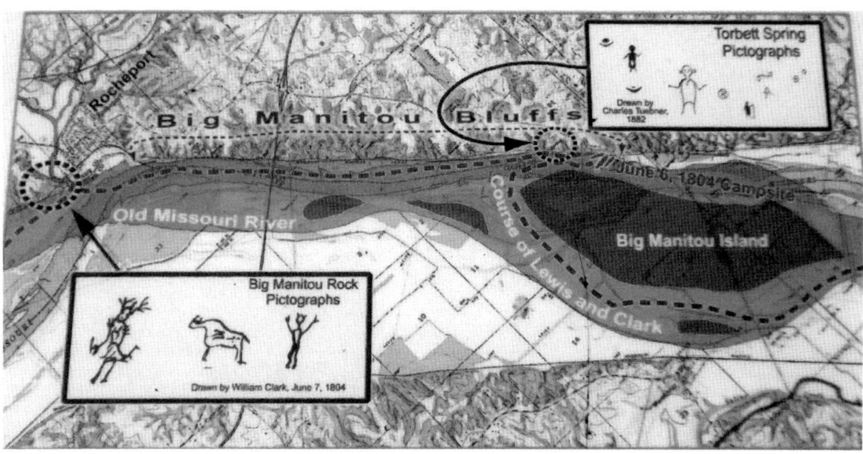

This map shows where pictographs and petroglyphs were found along the Missouri River near Rocheport.

and slit the moccasin soles to make it difficult for a ghost to walk back to the camp. Because ghosts could cause famine, a lump of fat was placed in the hand of the dead to provide them with food. Ghosts were known to whistle, and people feared anyone who made that sound. If a person fainted, she was thought to have visited the spirit world and been forced to return because she was not yet ready for the next plane.

Author Washington Irving, who stayed in Columbia on his way to the prairies in 1832, recorded an Osage story about ghosts: A young brave returns from a trading journey to St. Louis with gifts for his future wife. He discovers the camp has been abandoned, but his love is waiting for him. She has been weeping and avoids his embrace but tells him where the tribe has gone. The couple travel to the new camp, the girl carrying their pack, but she is quiet and draws her robe closely around her. The young man runs ahead to the camp and calls greetings to his family. They are subdued, and his sister finally reveals that the brave's wife-to-be had died and was buried beneath a nearby tree. The brave, knowing he had just traveled with his love, runs to the tree, discovers his pack on a newly dug grave and dies from grief.

CHILDREN'S GHOSTS

Some ghost stories are as evanescent as their subjects, with little to offer except the "what" and the "where"; very often the "who" and the "why" were forgotten long ago. But that hardly makes the ghosts less strange, seeking, as we do, to understand our own futures, the way a dust mote seeks a sunbeam. The following are stories about children who left this earth much too early. At least, that is what we tell ourselves.

THE POND

Today, visitors who wander south of town can still glimpse a bit of what the country was like a century ago. If they take a turn here and a curve there, they will come across the Old Plank Road. It leads down the bluffs to Perche Creek and the abandoned Providence steamboat landing. Legend has it that, in 1840, a lanky young man named Abraham Lincoln hiked up from the landing and into Columbia to visit a lady friend, Miss Mary Todd, who was visiting cousins in the muddy, bustling village of Columbia. The *Columbia Evening Missourian* carried a story in 1920 about the Plank Road, noting that it was among the first of its kind in the state. The road was built in 1853 from split planks, which provided a firm footing over muddy ground but also resulted in a jostling and bumping ride of several miles in a lightweight hack. It was not unknown for visitors

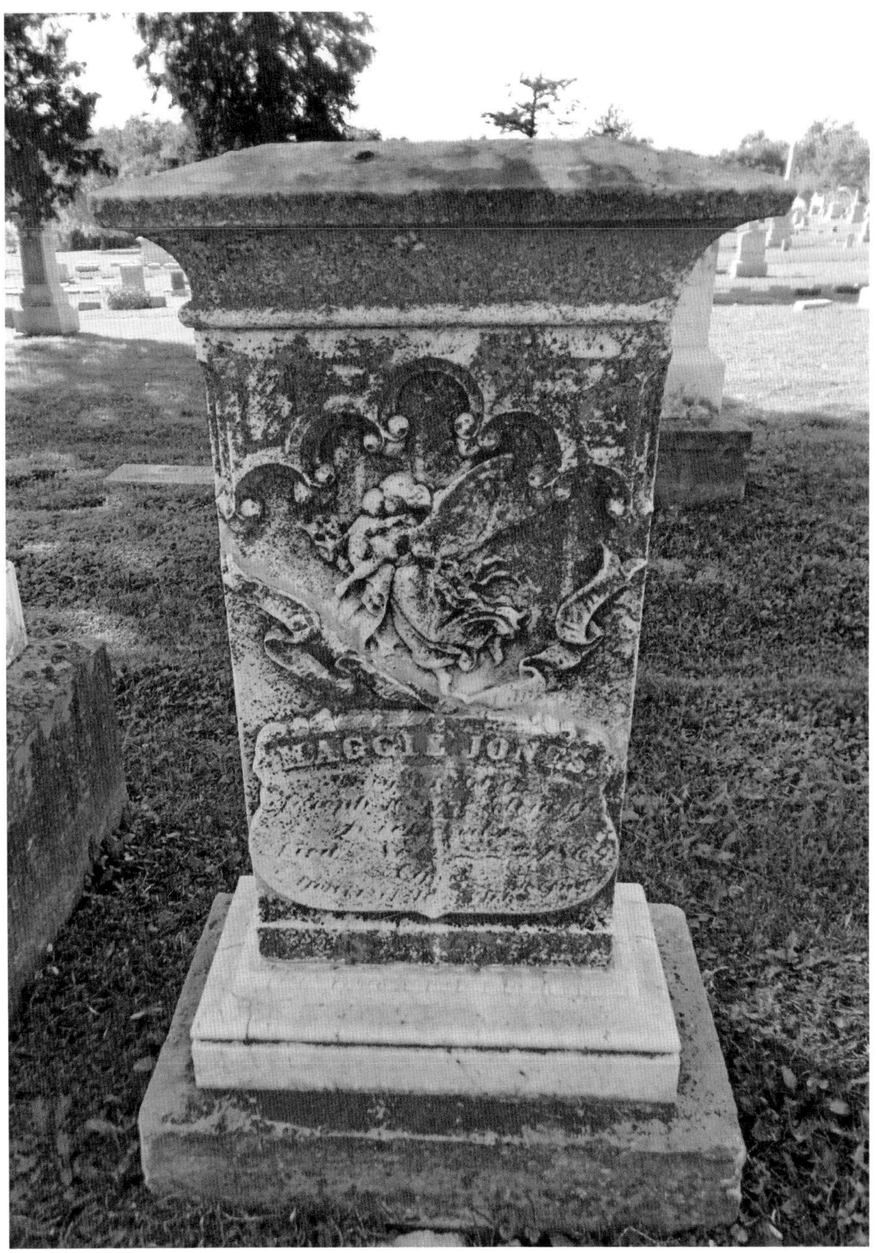

This gravestone, for a young child, depicts an angel carrying the soul to heaven.

to begin their journey in good humor and arrive in town unable to feel much beyond their headaches.

For generations before the Civil War and well into the twentieth century, the land along Old Plank Road was agricultural and bordered by fields and meadows. The farms held dairy and beef cattle, field crops and orchards. Farmhouses were built nearby the road for easy access, and there were ponds for livestock, fishing and fire protection. One farm on Old Plank Road had two ponds: a larger one, shaped like an old-fashioned hourglass, and a second pond, more commonly rounded but deep. Ponds could be useful but also deadly for those who couldn't swim. The two ponds were popular with skaters and often used by children as a frozen playground. In the 1930s, one family suffered a winter's tragedy: Their young son ventured too far out on the ice when alone at home. His body was discovered hours later, and the accident was forgotten by all but the family and people who passed by every day.

In the 1980s, the farm's land was sold for development, and large homes on small lots sprouted in the fields like teasels. The ponds remained, a boon to owners who could satisfy insurance company demands for nearby water sources in the event of brushfires or worse. There, heron still stalk bullfrogs, and in spring, the ponds are bordered by maypops and honeysuckle. But evening's dark is a different time and place on the small pond. Particularly in the winter's moonlight, a small shadow will appear over the water, and the scratching of metal can be heard—an awkward sound of old skates on rough ice. No matter how hard one looks, the shadow has no definition, no details—just movement. Then comes a tearing crack and, finally, silence. Whether or not there is ice, the shadow figure floats over the water, repeating that awful afternoon eighty years ago. The scene has been played out over generations and reported by visitors. It is not known if the current owner is aware of the ghost, but that has never stopped the spirit, heedless of this world.

THE GIRL ON THE BRIDGE

Hauntings are rarely extensive events: a glimpse, a cry, can reveal in a split second a terrifying story with no beginning or end. We rarely know why a haunting occurs or what brings a spirit back to earth. One teenager never forgot his encounter on a bridge west of Columbia. It still haunts him decades later.

It was about fifteen years ago, and a bunch of us were hanging out one night in summer near the river, at the old bridge. We were sitting on benches, and from there you could see across the bridge. It was starting to thunder, and we knew we were going to get soaked if we didn't leave. I stood up to go and looked up the road onto the bridge. I couldn't believe what I saw—and my friend, he saw it too. About fifty feet along on the bridge there was a little girl—oh, say, seven or eight years old—standing all alone. We had enough light for me to see that she was wearing all white. Kind of a dress . . . looked real old-fashioned. Her hair was down her back and blond. I've got kids of my own today, and when I think back, I know what I saw. My friend and me, we looked at each other and then started onto the bridge. We were afraid that the kid was lost or that she had been in an accident. We called out "Hey!" to get her attention, but she just walked over to the railing. By that time, we knew something was wrong, and we started running. It wasn't, oh, say, thirty feet, but it felt like forever. We yelled for her to wait for us, but she just pulled herself onto the railing. I screamed at her to stop, and that's when she turned her head and looked straight at us. Just a blank look, like we weren't there. Then she pushed off and dropped off into the water. I couldn't believe it. I don't know how it happened, but I saw it. By the time we got to the

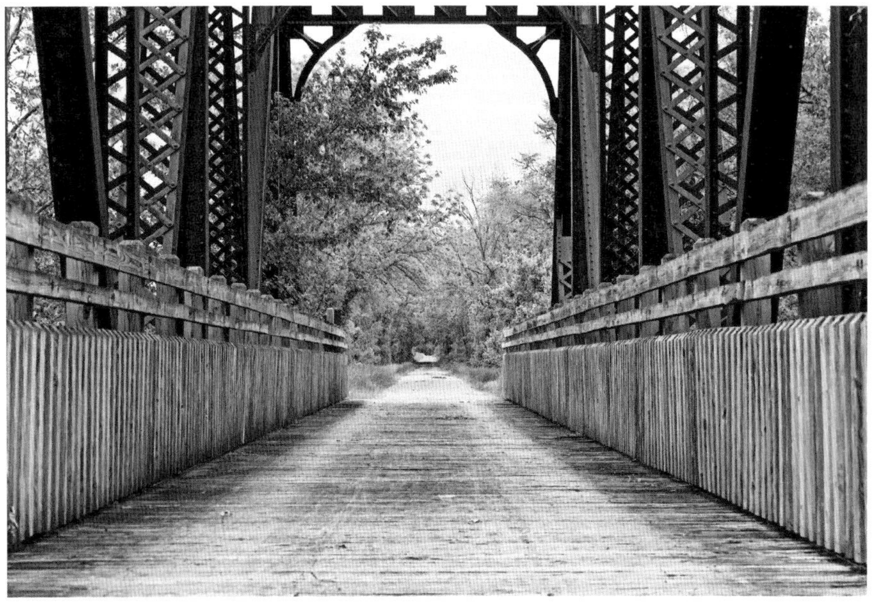

A bridge near Columbia. *Photograph by Tina Edholm.*

spot, she was gone. Then all hell broke loose with rain and lightning. The bunch of us, we ran two blocks to the police station. They didn't believe us at first, thought we were pulling their leg or something, but they sent a cop with a spotlight to look. Nobody saw or heard anything. I checked a few weeks later. No one found a body. No one reported a kid missing. One of my friends knew a cop and found out that the police had an earlier report of a little girl in white playing on the riverbank under the bridge. They didn't see anything when they went to look. My friend still won't talk about it. If I try to bring it up, he just shakes his head. "Nope. Not that. I'm not going there," he says. "No way."

HAUNTED CABIN ON THE PRAIRIE

This event was experienced by weekend residents who had no idea what they were getting into when they purchased their dream home.

We bought the house [south of Columbia] *because it was really old, but we didn't realize part of it was a log cabin until we started doing renovations and pulling down the walls. It seems the back part of the house was the original cabin, and the front was added later. We were pretty excited to see the squared-off logs and the pieces of wood shoved in between to hold the mud chinking in place. It cost us a lot to repair, but it was worth it in the end. Not many people can say they live in an original log cabin. We went there every Friday and back on Sunday evenings. Not a long drive, but you felt like you were out in the middle of nowhere. It was really quiet there at first. Then one night, I woke up and heard a baby crying. My wife heard it, too. We thought it was an animal outside, you know, like a rabbit and an owl, so we ignored it the first couple of times and figured that we had to get used to the night sounds out in the country. Then there were a few weeks when we didn't hear a thing. But not long after that, my wife woke me up, and we listened to that baby for a good half hour. It just didn't stop crying, and it wasn't hysterical, you know, like when kids have a tantrum? Just a constant wailing and crying. It kind of faded out as we listened, like it was moving away from the house. I look out the window, but there was absolutely nothing I could see, and by then it was completely silent. I don't think either of us slept any more that night. I can't say we got used to the crying, but what were we supposed to do? Call the police? Some of our guests heard it when they stayed over. Not as loud as we heard, but enough to mention it to us in the morning. Then one afternoon, we were walking around our field with some friends; it was early winter, so there weren't any leaves on the trees, and you could see better. One of the group noticed a stone or a shape under some bushes, and once we cleared away the brush, it turned out to be a headstone. There were a few of them, up against the end of the field and the woods, and you could see this had been a small cemetery, probably for the people who lived out here. The headstone had a lamb on it, for a young child or a baby. The name on the stone was "Anna" with no dates. Just "Anna." We came back the next day and cleared the area a bit so that now you can see the graves. We go out there every now and then and make sure nothing's been disturbed. The crying has stopped, at least for the past few months. Maybe we were hearing the wind. Maybe it was an animal. I just don't know what it was. But I'm sure of something: there's one place I won't be at dark, and that's out in the field.*

Ghosts and Logs

Taverns once dotted the Boonslick Trail from the Mississippi River to Franklin, offering travelers a place to stop and rest. The frontier taverns provided what they could in the way of food and facilities; two or three strangers might find themselves sharing a bed with fleas and bedbugs for the night. Noah Ludlow, an actor and writer who traveled the backwoods in the 1830s, recalled stopping with fellow actors at a tavern, where they shared a small room with two boisterous boatmen. The actors couldn't sleep for all the drunken shouting, and they knew they had to get rid of their roommates. Ludlow and his friends waited until the boatmen were asleep, then one tiptoed out of the room with a sheet. Suddenly, with a crashing of doors and chairs, the "ghost" of Hamlet's father appeared in the room. The actors cried loudly for help, waking the boatmen, who fled in terror, never to be seen again. The acting troupe slept well the rest of the night.

Until recently, the only remaining tavern on the Boonslick Trail was Van Horn's Tavern, a log building where poor and rich alike stopped for supper and a bed. The tavern was typical for its day, with two sections connected by a breezeway. The rooms were about twenty feet square, with dining areas downstairs and beds upstairs. Food was served, and drinks included rum, whiskey and cider—guaranteed to make the evening fly by and the beds seem cleaner. Among the stories told around the fire were tales of ghosts. But this one may have been too close to home to allow the listeners a dreamless rest, since the setting was, in fact, Van Horn's Tavern.

The story goes that a traveler woke the house one night by screaming that the tavern was haunted. His fellow travelers calmed him enough to hear his story. After he fell asleep, he was yanked back to consciousness when the bedclothes were pulled off his bed. He replaced them, only to have the blankets pulled down once more. On the third time, the man held on to the blankets as an unseen being pulled with all its might and won the contest. Then the man heard sobbing and weeping in the corner of the room, saying that it sounded like a child in pain. Finally, a small, white figure floated up the wall, and the traveler fled the room in terror. Very soon, the tale had traveled up and down the trail, and the landlord was unable to rent the room. He decided to try to spend the night there to disprove the story, but as soon as he fell asleep, the blankets were tossed away, and a ghostly figure sobbed around the room. From that night on, the landlord locked the door and resigned himself to the loss of income.

One cold night, a circuit-riding minister stopped at the tavern. The landlord had no room at all for him, unless the minister wanted to stay in the haunted room. The minister, being a man of God, said he was not afraid of any spirits and would gladly take the room rather than the cold barn. The landlord showed the minister to bed, and the reverend had barely settled down and extinguished the candle flame when his blankets flew across the room. Shocked at first, this minister quickly remembered that a ghost must answer if addressed in the name of the Lord. Calling out, "What do you want, in the name of God?" the minister heard a child's voice from inside the wall: "I want a Christian burial. I cannot rest." The minister was frightened but promised the ghost that he would try to find the body and hold services to ensure eternal rest. The spirit quieted immediately, and the minister slept the rest of the night in peace.

The next morning, the minister reported what had happened in the night, and workmen tore a hole in the room's plaster wall, uncovering a terrible secret: the remains of a child. Apparently, no one could identify the child, so the minister dug a grave under the trees and consigned the child's body to eternity and peace. The discovery finally brought forth a confession: a workman who had been plastering the walls while the tavern was being built was approached by a vagrant child for food. The man said no; when asked by the boy again, the man struck blindly, killing the boy. In a panic, he placed the child's body into the wall space and hid his crime by plastering over the evidence. There is no record that the workman paid for his crime, but the tavern was never troubled again by a ghost.

PETER PAN AND CAPTAIN SPOOK

Stephens College, established in 1833 as the Columbia Female Academy, has, over the past 180 years, contributed to the cultural and educational life of the city. The college's hauntings are famous, too, including the Civil War story of a young woman and her Confederate soldier lover who were discovered together. According to one of many versions, the man was executed by Union troops, and the woman killed herself in despair. She is said to haunt several Stephens buildings, eternally searching for her lover. Unfortunately for the legend, there are no records of these deaths or of anything connected with an execution and suicide at Stephens.

Evidence or not, at least one group has had an experience that remains difficult to explain. According to a 1971 story in the *Columbia Tribune*, it was Halloween when students, a teacher, several guests and a newspaper reporter gathered in Senior Hall, hoping to see the abovementioned ghosts. The story noted that the closed room suddenly filled with wind, which blew out the only candle. Journalist Bob M. Gassaway recalled:

> *There was the sound of slow steps at first. When they stopped, deep breathing became audible. . . . I waited for the person to come through the door. And waited. And waited . . .* [so] *I moved to the hallway. . . . Halfway down the hall, I saw the figure of a man. Then the swish of a woman's long skirt caught my eye as the man dropped into a half crouch, his left hand outstretched as though to ward something off. Then both figures disappeared down the stairs.*

The rattled witnesses quickly shared notes and left the building, having gotten much more than they expected. Hours later, the teacher received a phone call from students who had not been with the group. The young women reported that a woman in a gown stopped them outside of Senior Hall and told them that the teacher was no longer welcome in the building. It was a warning best heeded by sundown.

Another Stephens ghost is much more decorous and still eternally dedicated to the school. Stephens has long been famous for its theater department, which produced many Broadway and film performers. What is less known is that the department was founded by Maude Adams, muse and friend of playwright J.M. Barrie and the actress who defined Peter Pan onstage. Nearly forgotten today, only a century ago Adams was the highest-paid actor in the country, inspiring adoration from audiences. Although Maude died in 1953, she has never quite left the Stephens campus.

Maude Adams was born in 1872 in Salt Lake City, Utah, to Annie Adams and James Kiskadden. Her mother was a popular actress and a favorite of Mormon leader Brigham Young and his family, while her father had lived a wild life in the American West until settling down. Annie and James married against her family's wishes, and she retired from the stage until after Maude's birth. Annie soon tired of her husband's drinking and returned to acting, taking Maude with her. Maude received little formal education before the age of ten and left school at fourteen, gaining a reputation as a natural stage presence. In 1889, under the guidance of impresario Charles Frohman, Maude achieved immense success on the Broadway stage, until Frohman's death in 1915 on the *Lusitania*. (Frohman refused to take a lifeboat seat, instead standing aside for others and quoting Peter Pan's lines, "Why fear death? It is the most beautiful adventure in life." On the night of his death, Frohman was seen by a company clerk, who discovered the impresario sitting at his desk—in New York. When the frightened man returned with other employees, Frohman was gone and the office dark. The company received news of his death the next day.)

Crushed by Frohman's death, Maude retired. But in 1935, President James Wood of Stephens College convinced her to come to Missouri to start the theater department. At Stephens, Maude was famous for her classes in breathing and vocal exercises. A demanding taskmaster, she was known for summoning the technical staff at 2:00 a.m. Students and staff quickly learned to disappear when they heard Maude's approach, her shoes making a distinct tapping sound up and down the halls. Adams lived for a time in the President's House on campus, treated like a queen, eccentric and brilliant, loved and respected by her students. She was closely associated with the old South Auditorium (torn down in 2004), the President's House and Senior Hall (both of which still stand).

As recently as the early 2000s, former "Stephens girls" still remembered Maude, calling her imposing and aristocratic. "We were terrified of her," recalled one. "She would demand constant work and dedication, but she loved what she did and we knew that." The student also remembered a rather unusual encounter in the 1960s:

> *I was in the auditorium, visiting the campus after several years away. It was evening, and I was waiting for a friend. Suddenly, across the floor, I heard those distinct footsteps—tap, tap, tap—and then heard Miss Adams's voice. I'm not certain what she was saying—I was too shocked to listen closely—but it was clear to me that she was teaching a class. That same repetition of nonsense syllables we always did. The sounds faded and it was all quiet again, and I left pretty quickly, I can tell you.*

Another student reported seeing the figure of a short woman wrapped in a cloak:

> *I was on the campus one evening in the 1970s, having returned for an alumni event, and was walking near the President's House. I remember that the lights were on in the house, and I thought how lovely it looked. During my day on campus, it was a tradition for us to stop in at the house if the lights were on, and we were always welcomed by President Rainey and his family. As I looked that night, a figure walked up the front stairs to the door. It was a short woman, and she had on a funny little cap. I saw her standing there, at the door, and then she stepped to the side, and I didn't see her again. She didn't walk down the steps, and I did not see the door open. If people didn't think I was nuts, I would have said without a minute's hesitation that it was Miss Adams.*

Other students have reported hearing Maude reciting from Shakespeare or the play *Chanticleer*, in which she starred on Broadway and which she directed at Stephens. One woman who pursued a theatrical career said that every time she was onstage, she felt that "Miss Adams was standing there with me. It wasn't wishful thinking—I just knew that she was making certain that I remembered all her breathing exercises."

Time Slips

Some of the most vivid ghost encounters occur as "time slips": an experience when someone sees the past as it was. It is the same effect as looking through an old-fashioned stereo viewer: the past is right there in front of you, in three dimensions, and then you look up and it's gone. You are back in your time. One of the most famous time slips involved Versailles, France, where two teachers reported stumbling into a garden party from the seventeenth century. Another occurred in 2004 in the Ozarks, according to author Jason Offutt, when a young man blacked out and came to an hour later. He seemed confused and asked his parents about the black president—four years before Barack Obama was elected. When time slips occur, they are unexpected, disorienting and as real as anything. In these stories, two Columbia residents share their time slips, which occurred in the 1970s and still confound the victims nearly a half century later.

Hunting the Past

My dad and I loved working together on the farm. It had been started just before the Civil War, and my grandfather bought it in the 1920s. We raised corn and other crops and did haying. We kept a few cows. Columbia was nearby, but you could see the stars like you were in the middle of nowhere. One summer evening, Mom and the girls were at a movie, so me and Dad decided to play cards with his friend Bob. I remember it was still kind of early, but there was enough light so we could mostly see across the fields. We were laughing and joking when Bob looked out and asked who was in the field that late. We all looked and saw a man walking around the field, about sixty yards from the fence. He had a gun and a dog with him, and you could see him stop and pet the dog. The man had a beard and wore a hat and jacket, which were too warm for summer. Well, we figured he was either lost or didn't have any business there hunting at dusk, so I went outside to check. I walked across the yard over to the fence, but there wasn't anyone I could see, and I figured he had headed home. When I got back in the house, Dad and Bob asked me what the man wanted. I said he was gone. "No, he's not. He's still there," and Bob pointed at the window. Well, there he was, and I could see the shape of a rifle over his shoulder and the dog running back and forth like he was getting a scent. The man took off his hat and scratched his head, but he didn't look over at the house. It was like we weren't even there. I went back out, but this time I grabbed my gun, called my dog from inside the house and headed into the field. I could see Dad and Bob pointing to where I should walk, but damned if there was anyone. My dog growled and backed up a bit, so I stopped but heard absolutely nothing. Then Dad and Bob showed up, and we stood

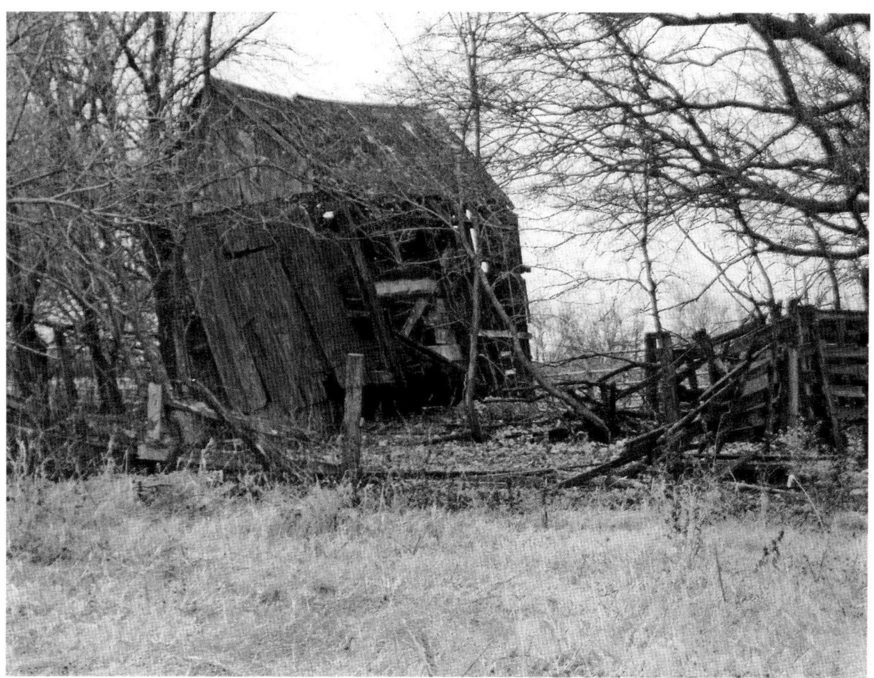

Derelict buildings are some of the most haunted places around Columbia.

there for a few minutes, really quiet, listening and looking around. You could see straight across the fields and into the trees. Nothing. We were all puzzled and kind of on edge since we had seen this guy with the gun not a few minutes ago. We headed back to the house and called our dog, who ran to the door. He didn't want any part of that field, and he was a hunting hound. We got inside and sat down again, trying to make sense of what just happened. Then we heard it: a rifle shot and a dog chasing something. Just outside the house, real close in the yard. We looked, and there was nothing. I can tell you, we waited up for the girls. It never happened again, but I know what I saw. And so did Dad and Bob.

House Party

In the 1960s, when I was about thirteen, my friend invited me to stay overnight at her aunt's house, which was near the business loop. It was an old farmhouse, since torn down, with two floors, lots of windows and a large yard with a barn. The barn had boards missing from its sides, but it was a great place to play, and we had a lot of fun jumping in the hay. I'm pretty sure my parents would have been horrified if they knew what we were up to around the farm equipment. That night, we each had our own room on the top floor, looking out on the yard. It was a nice old house, and after the long day, I fell asleep early. I'm not sure what time it was but I woke up because I heard a lot of horses in the yard. I was really excited since I knew there weren't any horses around there, and I thought maybe someone was riding through. I got up to look out the window. I saw a group of men and women. There were also horses and wagons. The men were dressed in some kind of uniform, and the women wore long skirts. I could hear the horses and voices, like someone was talking loud, but I don't remember any words. I watched everyone moving around the yard and the women greeting each other. I remember that I couldn't tell a lot of color or detail because it was still kind of dark with the dawn just starting. I called across the hall to my friend to come and see, but when I looked out again, there was no one. Everything was gone. My friend came in, and she didn't see anything, but I was wide awake and pretty wound up. Of course, when we went outside, everything was as usual. I wish I knew more about the house and its history. I know I was seeing something old, but to this day, I don't know what. If you asked me to guess, I would say Civil War. I had the feeling that the people were getting ready to leave. It was the oddest experience of my life.

The Ghost Music of John William Boone

John William Boone is still remembered for his contributions to early ragtime music, but he was also an influential classical pianist, musical genius, composer and humanitarian. Boone overcame hurdles high enough to stop most people: he was blind since childhood and black, the son of a former slave and a white musician. Even though there are no recordings of Boone performing, his distinctive sound has not disappeared from living memory, since at least two Columbians witnessed a most unusual concert.

John "Blind" Boone was born in 1864 in Missouri. His mother, Rachel Carpenter Hendricks, had been freed by Union troops and was determined to provide her son with a good life and an education. After the war, Rachel and John moved to Warrensburg, where she married and worked as a housekeeper. There, tragedy shadowed the family yet again: while still a toddler, John contracted a fever and was at the brink of death. One of the few treatments at the time for brain swelling was to remove a patient's eyes. John survived the operation, but little was expected for the future of a blind, poor and black child at a time not long before Jim Crow laws would take full effect.

Despite his blindness, John displayed a remarkable joy for life and music, playing intricate rhythms on homemade instruments, composing songs and singing them to playmates. Rachel's employer helped her send John to the school for the blind in St. Louis, where John discovered a piano, convinced an older student to give him lessons and soon made it clear that he was a gifted musician. John, like Mozart, could hear something once and replay

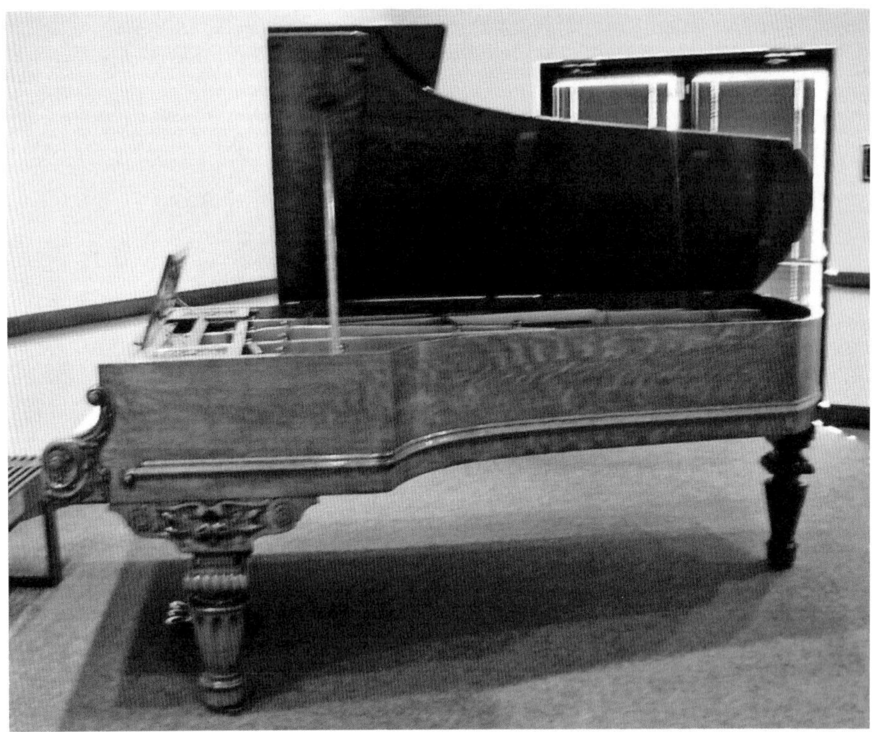

John William "Blind" Boone's piano.

any song or sound on the piano without errors. His music lessons ended when a new school superintendent thought John would be better served learning to make brooms.

John returned home, became a street performer and, as a teenager, was taken under the wing of John Lange Jr., a businessman and community leader. Lange and Boone's partnership resulted in fame and fortune, and Lange promoted his friend's talent on the idea that "merit, not sympathy, wins." Boone traveled the country, returning each time to a gracious frame house at 10 North Fourth Street in Sharp End, black Columbia's vibrant neighborhood.

There, Boone's piano had pride of place in the front parlor. A short man (five feet, two inches tall), he was powerful when he played music, wearing out sixteen pianos during his lifetime. Boone's last piano was a grand Chickering—a huge, sturdy oak instrument reinforced by a cast-iron frame. It had a rich, unmistakable tone, and when Boone played, the sound carried through the house and into the street, where neighbors enjoyed impromptu concerts from their porches. Among Boone's compositions were a few that would later be called "ragtime" as well as classical tone poems depicting, through the music, everything from rainstorms to military battles and spinning wheels.

Boone's career slowed drastically after the death of John Lange. By the time of his passing in 1927, Boone was nearly bankrupt, leaving little to his wife except the house and the piano. He was buried in the Columbia Cemetery, but there was no money for a headstone. The world's greatest black musician rested in anonymity but perhaps not in peace.

Boone's beloved Chickering piano was still serviceable and was donated to the Frederick Douglass School, which served the black community. For years, school assemblies were enlivened by songs played on the instrument, and eventually it was moved to the second floor and used in music classes. Then, in 1960, thirty-three years after Boone died, journalist Mary Paxton

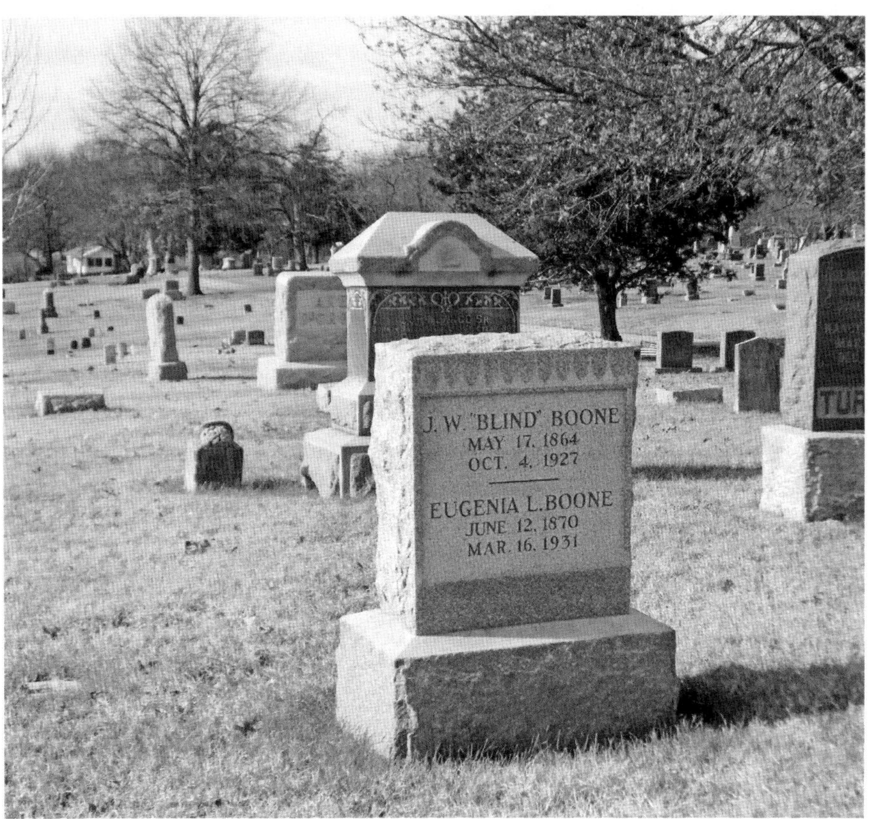

John and Eugenia Boone's graves.

Keeley interviewed Columbia resident Naomi Jones, who was asked her opinion of John Boone. "Oh, nobody else ever played like Boone," she answered. Keeley was confused. Boone had died in 1927, when Naomi was barely old enough to remember the music, and there were no phonograph records of Boone. She asked Naomi when she had last heard Boone, and the stunning answer was, "Last winter." Naomi recalled that "Vickie and me were going through the [Frederick Douglass] school grounds, about the time night was coming on, and when we were in front of the school house, Vickie stopped and said 'What's that, Mamma?' I stood and listened—'that's Boone playing, Vickie' and we stood there looking up at the dark windows where his piano stays, until he stopped playing." Naomi heard Boone on three separate occasions and could identify the ghostly songs, including ragtime and one of Boone's most technically difficult compositions, "The Marshfield Tornado." Naomi had no doubt that Boone's spirit was playing for her.

Naomi also knew that Boone wanted something from the living: a headstone to mark his grave. It was during this time that the Chickering piano was removed from the school for repair, after which it served as the centerpiece of a fundraiser for the headstone. However, that concert was a financial failure, and the piano was given to one of the organizers as security until he was paid.

As for the piano played by a ghost? It was sold to the Pierce City Masonic Lodge for $864 and remained there until 1971, when it was identified, refurbished and returned to Columbia, where it can be seen and heard at the county historical society. Boone's grave and that of his wife, Eugenia, were finally graced with headstones. Vickie, a grandmother, still remembers the night when a child and her mother heard music from the other side.

Conjuring Evil

This story shows the dangers of invoking spirits and asking for trouble: the results can be real or unreal. The tale was shared by a woman who lives just northwest of Columbia, down a gravel road in the country.

One of my friends was married, and her husband ended up in jail. I felt sorry for her and invited her to stay with me and my kids so she wouldn't be alone the year her husband was away. I live in a house about a quarter mile off the main road, with fields and woods all around. It's a great place, and we're so used to the wildlife, even the dogs just sit on the deck and watch the deer and possums. The place is so quiet, we don't lock the doors, and it's pretty rare to see any strangers on the road. One morning, my friend got a call from the prison warden telling her that her husband had suddenly passed away. It was terrible. We were all pretty shocked since he had been in good health, but once we all calmed down, she said she would spend the day making arrangements for the funeral two days later. Well, that night I came home from work, walked in the house and found her with lighted candles all around and the house in darkness. I asked what was going on, and she told me she was trying to contact her husband one last time. I don't hold with any of that nonsense, so I told her to stop it and never do anything like that again. Instead of apologizing, she said it was too late and that he was there. I figured it was all the stress, so after we calmed down, I made some tea and then went to bed.

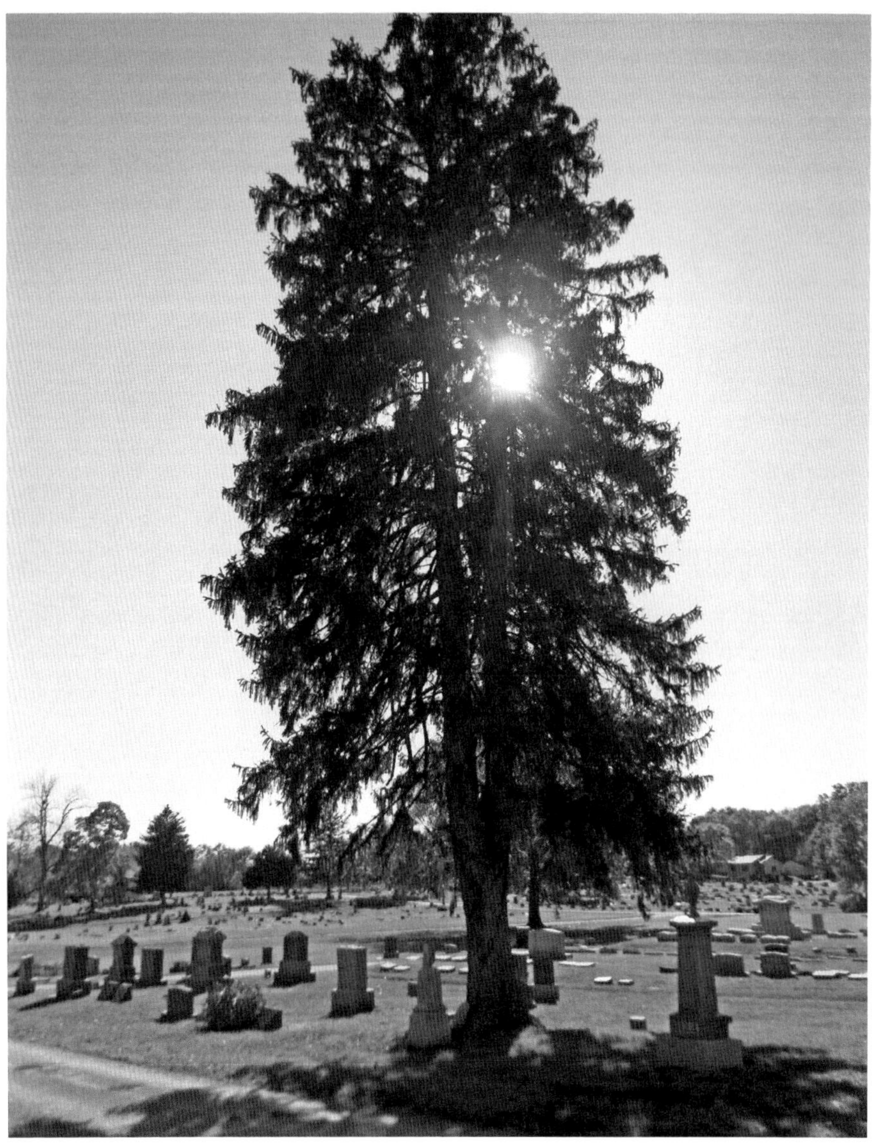

Restless spirits may sometimes find peace after formal interment.

A few hours later, I woke up to loud, continuous banging on the side of the house. I had no idea what it was, but I got up fast and looked out the window. The dogs were barking, and I have security lights, but they hadn't turned on until I stepped onto the deck. My friend had gotten up, too. She was real quiet but finally said, "It's him." I saw nothing, so I got the kids settled in their rooms and then got back to sleep. The next morning, I looked at the house for dents or damage, but there wasn't anything out of place. An hour or so later, I was taking the kids to school when we saw the high grass alongside the drive waving back and forth, like a deer was moving through. I stopped the car to let the deer get ahead of us, but nothing came onto the road. The grass was perfectly still. But as soon as I started driving, the grass swayed and the movement followed us until we reached the main road. Looking back, it was something I should have paid attention to.

When I got back to the house later that afternoon, I parked the car and was on the deck when I realized the living room curtains were moving back and forth. I mean, they were moving like anything, and there wasn't a heating or cooling vent near them. I knew no one was in the house who should have been, so I called the sheriff's office. The deputy who showed up searched the house with me, but he didn't find anything. I pretty much sat up the whole night. The next day we were heading to the funeral when the same pounding started on the roof of the car, like someone throwing rocks. We were terrified but kept driving until it stopped and we got to the cemetery. There was no damage to that roof, and there should have been, given all the banging. The service went fast, but as they were lowering the coffin into the grave, it fell to one side and thudded to the bottom. The funeral home apologized, but all I wanted to do was see the last of my friend and her husband. She moved out the next week, and I've had no disturbances since. I don't know about her. But me? I believe in all that ghost stuff. All of it.

The Women in Black and White and Gray

All roads are haunted by the stories of people passing through, but some roads are more haunted than others. Route 66 has its ghosts. Zombie Road terrifies hikers. But it is often the unknown, lonely, quiet places that can attract—or repel—the spirit. Among the most famous American road haunts is the white lady: a woman who asks for help and directs you to her home but when you get there all you find is an empty house or someone who tells you that "Susan" or "Abigail" or "Bessie" died years ago. Perhaps these ghosts are very old memories of La Llorona, "the weeping woman," a spirit from the southwestern and Mexican traditions who made her way up the Santa Fe Trail in the 1800s and never left. According to tradition, La Llorona is a woman who murdered her children and then herself but is denied a place in heaven until her children forgive her. She cannot find them, wandering the land dressed in white, crying and searching.

Missouri has at least two white ladies, in St. Louis and Boonville, but the state is also home to women in black who have darker tales to share. In Paris, Missouri, the Dark Lady's story began after the death of a village woman who was later seen and recognized by many people as she walked the town's streets after sunset, content with the night side of existence. According to a story in *The Haunting of America*, the woman was said to approach homes and look into windows, apparently intrigued by the children even as she terrified their parents.

Columbia contributes its own spirit to this group. A former resident recalled her encounter with the woman in black, still as vivid as the day it occurred.

> *It was a winter's afternoon, overcast, bitterly cold. My husband and I were driving along one of the roads west of town that winds out into the county. It was all farmland, as far as the horizon, with some old wire fences and completely empty. As we came around a bend, we saw an elderly woman walking on the shoulder of the road. She was dressed in black from head to foot. I remember she had on a long coat and a scarf or veil wrapped around her head and shoulders. In those few seconds, I got the impression she was crying and walking against the wind. After we passed her, my husband and I both said, "What the heck?" We figured she was lost or confused, and it was no day for her to be out there alone. In less than a minute, we had turned around the truck and headed back to check on her and offer her a ride. We went around the bend and then looked down the road—it was empty. We couldn't find an access road for nearly a half mile, and we drove up and down for more than a mile. No one. No nearby houses, there was no one in the fields, no opening in the fences and, anyway, how would that older lady climb the ditches in her long coat? She had disappeared in under two minutes. We even looked for footprints in the snowy patches and couldn't find a thing. It all happened so quickly but after I thought about it, I realized her clothing didn't make any sense. I know it sounds weird but I think we saw someone from another time, maybe the Civil War? I don't know. She was there, and we both saw her and she was gone. I still get chills when I think about her. She was so sad and alone. It's been a long time, and I still wish I knew where she was going.*

Closely related to the white ladies is the vanishing hitchhiker, who turns up now and again to befuddle drivers who stop to help. One of these eerie road companions made his way around the state in 1983, appearing along the roads from southeast Missouri to the Columbia area and north. One woman told of stopping to give a hitchhiker a ride against her better judgment, which she should have heeded: he asked her if she believed in God. When she said "Yes," he answered, "Good, because he's coming," before fading into thin air. The story goes on to say that she pulled over, shaking, only to have a state trooper stop and ask if she needed help. After calming down, she repeated what had happened, thinking the trooper would take her to a hospital. But he told her that he had been hearing the story from other drivers that same week.

COLUMBIA'S GRAY LADY

Columbia College was founded in 1851 as Christian Female College, the first women's school west of the Mississippi to be chartered by a state legislature. Ladies who wanted advanced education studied writing, Old Testament history, ancient geography, history, philosophy and arithmetic. Between classes, the women attended chapel, studied, helped with chores and composed daily essays. By 1856, Christian College boasted

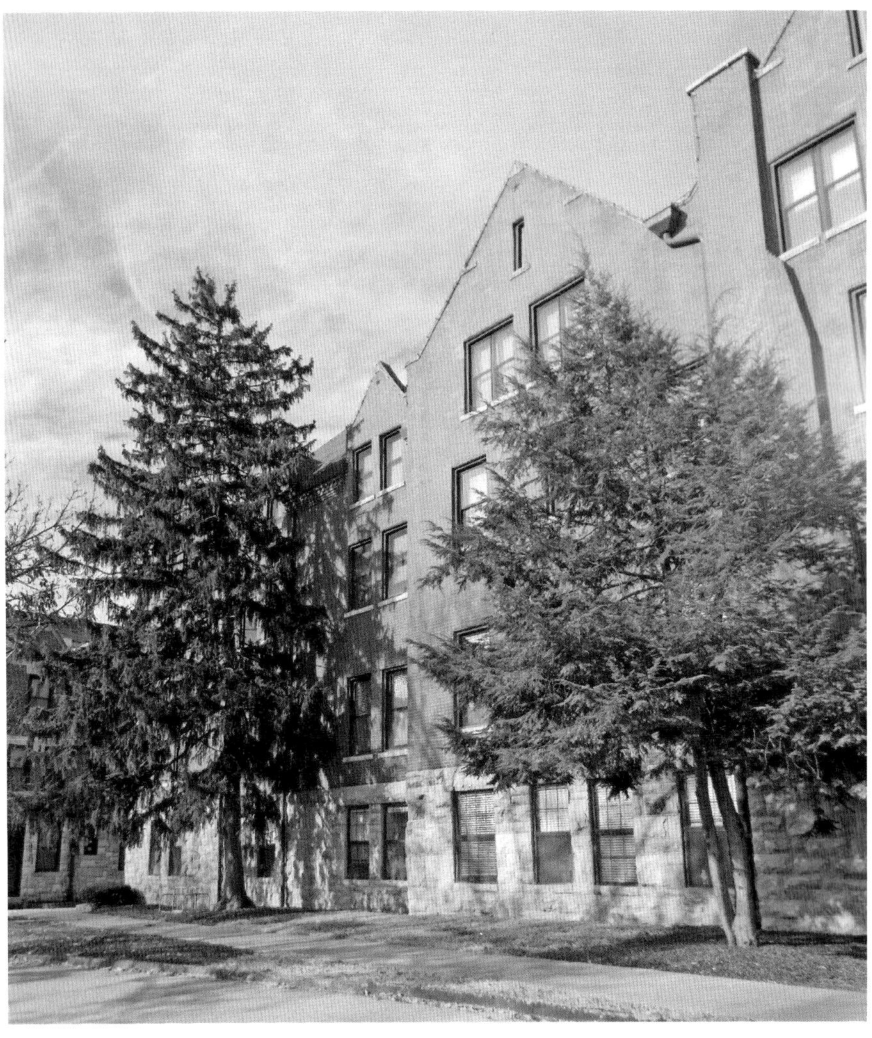

Columbia College was once the site of a well-known haunting hoax.

150 students. The Civil War presented the school with a difficult choice: while Columbia was pro-Union, the Little Dixie region around the college and city was filled with Southern sympathizers, so the college resolved to remain neutral as long as possible. Unlike many other institutions, Christian College did not close during the war, despite reduced attendance and graduation rates. Among the students was Lavinia "Vinnie" Ream, a sculptor and painter and the first American woman to receive an artist's commission from the U.S. government. After the war, the college expanded, and in the 1970s, it became a coeducational institution. Today, Columbia College is a vibrant learning community and cultural center. But at least one of its students who walks the halls has a long history there, far longer than any mortal could expect.

For generations, the story has been told of a Christian College student who killed herself over a lost love during the Civil War. But instead of resting in peace, the Gray Lady wanders the corridors of St. Clair Hall. She still cares deeply for her sisters and has been known to close windows, neaten desks and even iron clothing, all without acknowledgement. One drawback to the legend: St. Clair Hall was not constructed until the year 1900. But on a spring night in 1965, the legend received a new boost. Students crossing campus looked up at St. Clair's windows to see a white figure carry a candle across a room and then pass through the wall to continue its march. The observers were rooted to the spot, watching as the ghost made her way across the building, despite plaster and wood. When the dean of students heard the story, she immediately called for student Penny Pitman, a young woman known for her brains and sense of humor. The ghost was identified: Penny explained that she and a friend had wrapped themselves in sheets, carried candles and taken their places in different rooms. One woman glided across the room and then tapped on the wall, alerting the other woman to begin her walk. The effect from outside was of a figure drifting through solid plaster. Alas, the Gray Lady has not been seen much since that night but remains a cherished visitor who is, perhaps, just waiting for the right spring night.

PLEDGING TERROR

Fraternities and sororities all have ghost stories, but few have as many as Columbia's Greek houses. Described here are a few spirits who refuse to graduate.

GRASSLANDS GHOST

Phi Kappa Psi owns a grand old building on Providence Road, set back from the busy street behind a stone wall, gracious and timeless. This was the old Grassland Plantation, which had its beginnings when the Rollins family, led by father Anthony Wayne Rollins, immigrated to Columbia from Kentucky in the 1830s. The Rollinses' first home was a 1,200-acre plantation, purchased for $6,000 and called Richland. The family's influence continued into the next generation with Anthony's son James Sidney Rollins, father of eleven children and a Columbia lawyer, educator and businessman. James Rollins owned extensive property in Columbia, including the site of the future University of Missouri. He helped raise the enormous sum of nearly $118,000 to secure the university's establishment in Columbia, and he remained a leader of the university for another generation. Rollins lived in Columbia at his farm, LaGrange. (The original home, located at 512 Rollins Road, burned down in 1908.) Among the largest slave owners in the region, the family thrived, and Rollins later divided his land between two sons, George Bingham and Curtis, for the selling price of "one dollar and love and affection," as stated in the associated abstract. It was George Bingham, named after the artist and Rollins family friend George Caleb Bingham, who finally established the Grasslands farmhouse in 1880, which is still located at 809 South Providence Road. According to a *Columbia Tribune* article published in 1991:

> *George Rollins built the original house* [in 1880] *and three cabins. One . . . was a carriage house, another was a kitchen and the third cabin was an ice house. Some of the rocks of a wall built around the plantation property by employees and hauled by hand, rock by rock from near the present day Katy Trail, have been relocated to outline the fraternity driveway and parking lot. The barns and stables were on land now cut through by a street named Burman Road, west of Providence Road. A stepping stone, still in place, and once used for the convenience of carriage traffic, indicates that the elevation of the driveway has been raised. The stone is inscribed with the name of the home.*

Native Missouri trees sheltered the property, and the home was one of the loveliest in the city. Unfortunately, the home did not provide the same fortune for the children as it did for the parents: George Bingham Rollins was killed on June 18, 1915, when he fell into an abandoned well while testing the strength of some rotten cover boards, and his children inherited the house and land. In 1934, George's son Frank Bingham Rollins Jr., forty-eight years old and an insurance executive, a grandson of James Rollins, was killed at the home by a "self-inflicted gunshot wound, accidental," according to his death certificate. The house was sold to a local doctor in 1939. Finally, Phi Kappa Psi purchased the building in 1954 and continues to own it, although extensive renovations have been made to the structure over the years.

As with any home that has seen its share of tragedy, the Grasslands house has been reported as a host of hauntings through the years. Wynn Wiegand, a fraternity alumnus, told a reporter for the *Maneater* that he had experienced supernatural events when he lived there. "There were a lot of late night noise . . . some of which was not attributable to the creaking of an old house. . . . We heard footsteps when nobody was supposed to be in there." One other event remained in the memories of brothers who lived in the house in the 1980s. "It was over Christmas [break, and there was] snow on the ground," recalled Wiegand. The men heard banging on the front door, so they got up and went downstairs, where they found footprints leading to the front door but none leading away. Another story, less common but still shared, was about a child who was playing at the Grasslands. She chased a runaway ball on to Providence Road and was struck by a car and killed. Her ghost has been reported on the street, running into traffic to the terror of drivers, only for them to stop and find nothing amiss and no one around.

SISTERS IN GHOSTS

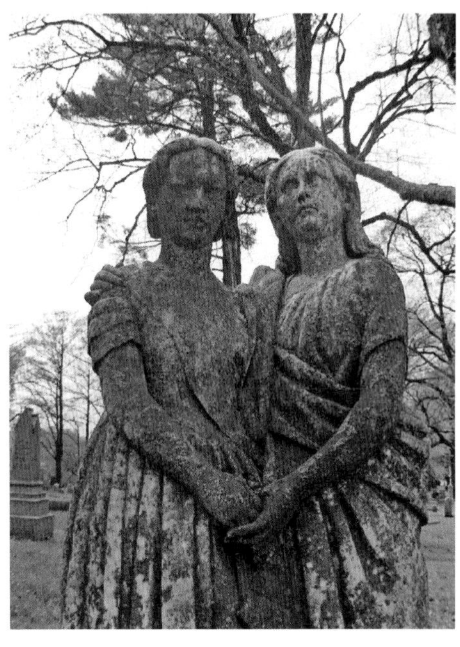

This memorial to a young woman who passed away while in school was erected by her sorority sisters.

At least one MU sorority has had its share of hauntings over the past forty years, by a ghost who has appeared variously as a young boy, a woman and a man, dressed in white and moving silently through the house. When the ghost is around, objects have been seen to fly through the air, strange smells waft through the halls, lights dim, doors slam and window shades snap up without warning. Although most of the sisters are not frightened by the ghost, one woman reported being pushed to the ground, and another said that she woke to feel someone sitting down on the bed when she was sleeping. Others say they see a reflection of a person in their mirrors but there is no one in the room when they turn around. The ghost was nicknamed "Chester," and stories of his appearances were passed down from mother to daughter. Perhaps he is still maintaining his silent vigil over the building.

Home Again

A-Haunting They Went

The *Professional World* newspaper was one of the few serving the black community of Columbia in the early twentieth century. Established by Rufus Logan in 1901, *Professional World* continued as a self-supporting news source for more than nineteen years, unusual for a paper that had to compete with white-owned companies for advertising. On August 1, 1902, the paper reported on a black-shrouded specter terrifying the neighborhood, albeit this ghost seemed to stir up more questions than horror. The tongue-in-cheek reporting masks a deep belief in spirits that was still found in Missouri towns:

> *Columbians have been stirred up for the past 10 days over the mysterious appearance of a being dressed in a black shroud, walks about at the still hours of midnight. There are many different theories presented regarding this strange visitor. Some seem to think it is a man dressed in woman's clothing and it is his intention to burglarize homes, while others claim that it is simply the intention of the plutonian caller to amuse himself by frightening the inhabitants of certain homes. While still others who consider the matter more seriously are confident that "it" is a supernatural being and is the forerunner of a great calamity that is to befall Columbia and are spending all of their spare time on their knees and calling on neighbors to straighten up all former differences. Some think also that since the midnight stroller is seen principally in the vicinity of the Fred Douglass school, that*

"it" is a sequence of the memorable school war recently ended here. With all of the theories and opinions passing around, little else has been discussed in the past week. And the question is now what can be done to rid the community of such a pest. The police were called to the scene by telephone last Monday night and soon opened fire on the departing figure, but the shots took no effect and the "ghost" made good his escape. Crowds of men have scoured the haunted section of the city for the past few nights, but have failed to capture "it" thus far. But it is evident that no peace will be had until "it" is captured.

FIRE AND FEAR

No one wants to experience a bad haunting. There is a great difference between seeing a lovely lady in a white gown drift through a room and feeling the cold and anger of something invisible. The latter happened to one young woman who lived on the family farm just outside the city of Columbia. She shared her story in a 2015 interview with the author.

My family owned the land since before the Civil War, and we still live there although the house was built later, in the 1880s, I think. Granpa, my mom's father, lived with us, and we were terrified of him as kids. He didn't talk much, and I don't think he ever laughed or joked. He kept busy hunting and trapping most days. He had a big shed that was up against the fields. That's where he kept his traps. I hated the place. There were always dead rabbits and squirrels hanging out there. It was always cold and dark there. The horses hated it, too. They would never go near the shed, and you had to walk them past it, or they would rear and kick. Granpa had some hunting dogs, big hounds. They lived behind the shed and never came near the house. I was about ten when Granpa died. About a year later, we woke up to hear the dogs barking and see the shed on fire. It burned to the ground, and my dad cleaned up the area. But the horses were still terrified of that corner. We kept the dogs, but they finally ran away. I guess they missed hunting.

Then last year, my boyfriend and I were outside. It was a real nice fall night, and we were looking at the stars. Suddenly, I smelled smoke and saw a big bonfire in the middle of the field. I told my boyfriend I was going to go over and see who was there. I had to cross where the shed had been and climb over the rail fence. I could see the flames not a few hundred feet away,

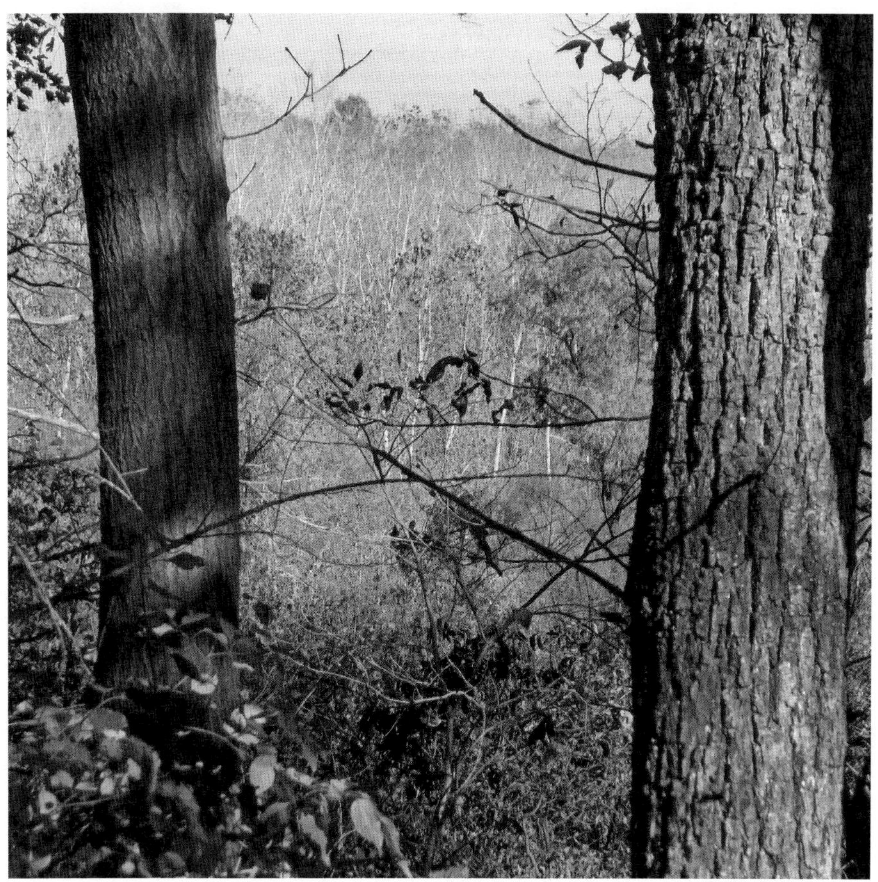

Missouri's landscape of deep forests and open prairies provides excellent settings for ghost stories.

but when I started over the field, the flames would die down. My boyfriend said he could see them, clear as anything, so he called out where to head. I got to where he said, but there was nothing: no smoke, no flames. He could see them, but I couldn't. I finally got scared and ran back to the fence, when we heard the most awful sound of hounds or coyotes or something. It was a pack, and they were coming right at us. We ran for the house, and we could hear them behind us, running and yowling, but we got inside and slammed the screen door behind us. The pack ran right by the house, you could see them clear as day, but there was nothing out there. It finally got quiet, and we locked all the doors and pretty much sat up that night. I don't know what we saw and heard that night, but whatever it was, it wasn't human. I won't stay there alone, ever.

TIME AND AGAIN

Ghosts sometimes attach themselves to families. In Ireland, a banshee cries when a member of certain families is about to die. In Scotland, there is the washerwoman who cries as she cleans the shroud for a person who is going to pass on. In Missouri, it was something very different for a woman from Columbia, who is still visibly moved when she shares her story.

> *My mother was an active and happy woman all her life. After my father died, Mom lived on her own, but we were very close and talked several times a day. She always joked that I'd get tired of her and stop listening to her advice. As Mom got older, she wasn't capable of taking care of herself. I cared for her the best I could in my house, which was big with lots of bedrooms. I slept upstairs, and Mom had a room downstairs. She could call me when she needed something, but she also had an old-fashioned clock that chimed loudly and would remind me of lunch. Unfortunately, Mom finally had to move to a skilled care facility, but I visited her every day, and this went on for a few years. One night, I woke up, startled to hear someone yell my name in my ear. It was as clear as a bell. The dogs and cat were still sleeping, but I got up to see if there was someone outside. Suddenly, Mom's old clock started to chime, bong, bong, bong. The dogs got off the bed and ran downstairs, and I followed them. They were staring up at the ceiling in Mom's old room, just over the bed, and barking like they heard a mouse or something. It took me a few seconds to quiet them down when the phone rang. It was the nursing home, calling to tell me Mom had just passed away and asking me to come down. If all that wasn't enough to get you to believe in the next life, there's something else: after Mom moved out, I was putting the clock into the closet when the movement fell apart. It couldn't have chimed the night Mom died. It hadn't worked for years.*

ROCHEPORT

The village of Rocheport is located along a river bordered by limestone cliffs, two things that traditionally attract ghosts. A walk along the back streets of the village reveals yards decorated with bottle trees, once used to capture witches or evil spirits by trapping them within the glass containers. The tradition may have been brought to this country by African slaves and spread north to Missouri with migrants. But more important, Rocheport certainly has its share of ghosts.

ROCHEPORT POND

A family had an unforgettable encounter with ghosts one winter's afternoon when the mother and son were traveling on a back road between Columbia and Rocheport.

> *It was years ago, before all that development along the bluffs. It wasn't dark yet, but there was fog. I would say we were about a mile outside of town. We were chatting and heading out for shopping when my son said, "Mom, look at those people." He pointed, and I looked to my right and could see five or six people walking parallel to us deep in the woods. They moved carefully, slowly, around the trees, and you could see the fog around them. I think there were men and women, maybe six*

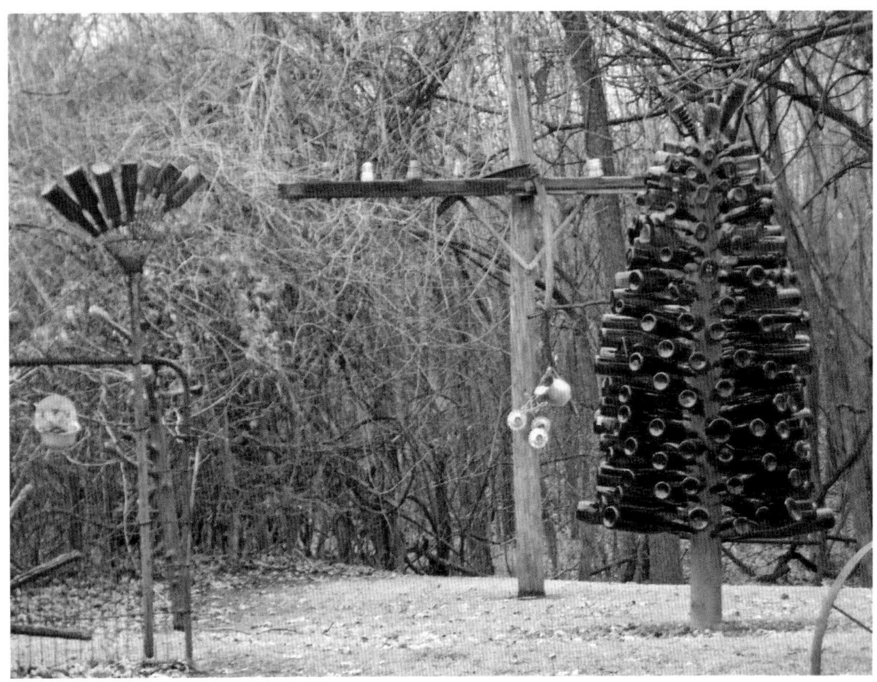

Bottle trees on a back street in Rocheport.

people total. The women had on hats and coats and long dresses, and the men were in trousers and heavy shirts. I pulled over to the side of the road, and we watched them get ahead of us and then angle over to the road, putting them in front of the car a few lengths up the road. They crossed the road, not looking around at all or paying us any attention, and as they got to the other side, they vanished. I don't know what else to say. They were there, and then they stepped off the side of the road and were gone. My son and I looked at each other and decided we didn't want to get out and look around. We drove into Columbia and took a different way home. All these years later, and I still don't know what I saw that afternoon. I asked around about who lived out there, but it was all grown-up woods, and no one knew of a family or other group. My son thinks we were seeing something from the past. I just don't know, and I'm happy I never saw them again.

KATY TUNNEL

Some built environments seem to attract hauntings or other activities, among them bridges and tunnels. What is it about those places that attract the sad or the dead? Sometimes the hauntings are associated with an accident; other times, the reason for the revenants is unknown. And perhaps that's for the best.

The Katy Trail State Park runs 240 miles across Missouri, following the rails of the old Missouri-Kansas-Texas (MKT) Railroad and passing by farmland, river bottoms, villages and towns. Despite its length, the trail has only one tunnel, at Rocheport in Boone County, west of Columbia. The Rocheport Tunnel was constructed in 1892, near the Moniteau Creek. This was near the Missouri River where, on June 7, 1804, William Clark noted in his journal that the Corps of Discovery had "set out early passed the head of the Island opposite which we Camped last night, and brackfast at the Mouth of a large Creek . . . Called big Monetou . . . a Short distance above the mouth of this Creek, is Several Courious Paintings and Carveing in the projecting rock of Limestone inlade with white red & blue flint, of a verry good quallity, the Indians have taken of this flint great quantities."

The manitou (also moniteau) is a life force, the Great Spirit as described by some Native American tribes. The "Courious Paintings" were rock paintings or petroglyphs, but who painted them and why remain a mystery, although they may date as early as 1000 CE. Four miles from the tunnel is the Big Moniteau art rock site, also called the Torbett Spring site. Here, petroglyphs include a number of figures, including beings with horns or horned masks, a bison, a crescent and dot, a figure holding a rod or a snake and perhaps Grandmother Spider. (These figures were described in 1881 by Charles Teubner and later by archaeologists Brownlee, Diaz-Granados, Duncan and Fuller.)

The Katy Tunnel has a strong connection to another dimension, at least as depicted in the film *Sometimes They Come Back*, based on a Stephen King story about ghosts gone very bad. The film was shot partly in Rocheport. The plot concerns a young boy who witnesses the death of local bullies in the tunnel as a train roars through; when he is a grown-up, he is visited by ghosts out for revenge. But in the real world, the visitations are even creepier, as in this story shared by the witness during an interview with the author in 2010.

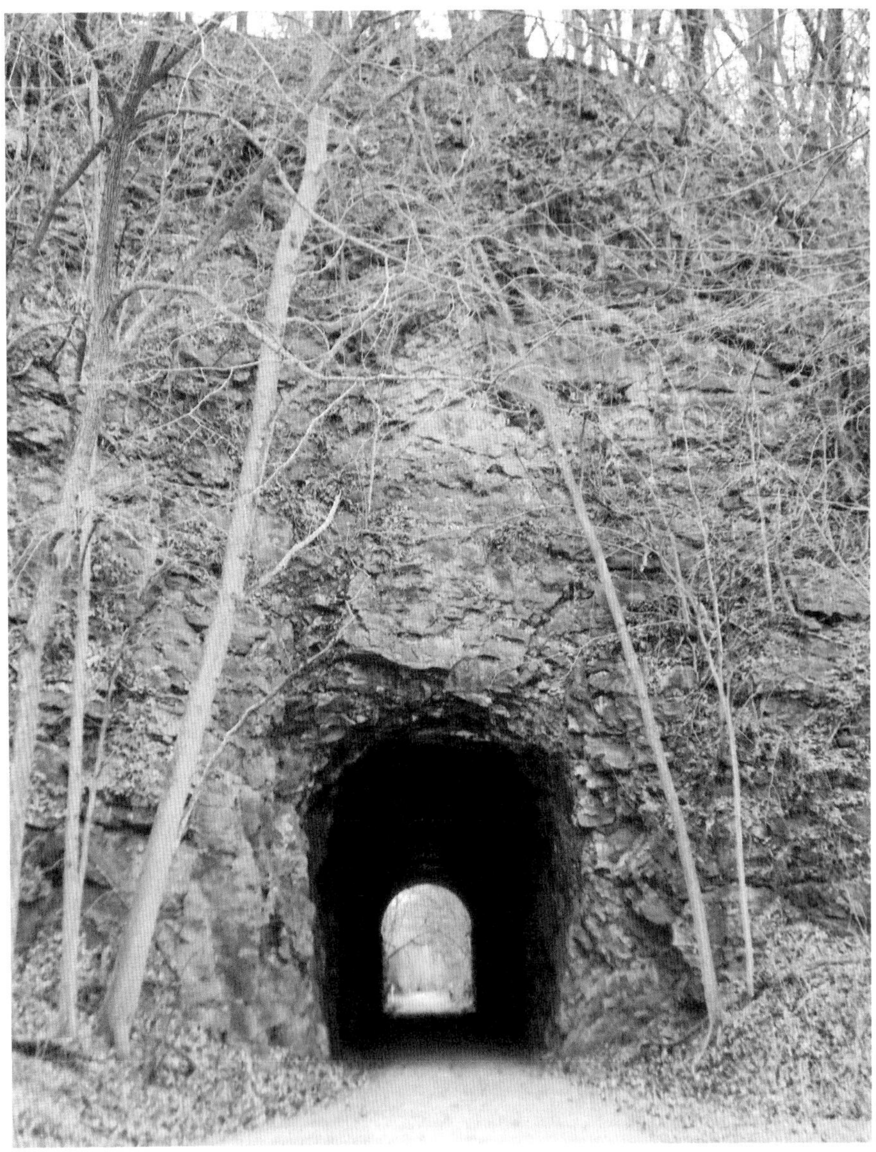

The Katy Tunnel in Rocheport appeared in a horror film adapted from a Stephen King story.

As kids, we always hung around the Rocheport tunnel, just because we weren't supposed to. Especially in the evening, but we would sneak out there to smoke and meet up with friends. This was the 1950s, and the trains were running. You could hear them coming miles off, and we would do things like put a coin on the rails so maybe it got flattened. It was supposed to bring you luck if you could find it later. Sometimes, we'd climb to the top outside and watch for the trains. The Katy was using diesels then, and they didn't slow down much through the tunnel. Just came rocking through and you could feel the wind. The noise was something awful. My Mom and Dad would've taken a belt to me if they knew I was that close to the trains. One night, we were around the tunnel, and we heard the train coming through. We all stood alongside the tracks. I was at the end of the line, and we were all joking and laughing. It was late summer, and still pretty light, and I could see the top of the tunnel. I looked up, and there was this figure. I don't know who it was. But he stood there for a second, holding a lantern or some kind of light, and before I could tell my friends to look, he was gone. I figured he was one of our friends and ran across the tunnel or slid down the side and was going to try and scare us. Then I looked through the tunnel and I saw him on the tracks. In the middle of the tracks with the light. He was walking away from us, and I pointed him out to my friend, and before we could say anything, here come the train. I nearly dropped dead, I can tell you. That train whooshed by, and all I could think was that the guy on the other side was a goner. It seemed like an hour before the train passed and we could run through the tunnel. Just as I got out, here comes one of our friends. I asked him if he was okay and asked why didn't he tell us he was on top of the tunnel and why would he cross in the middle of the tracks with a train coming? He looked at me like I had gone crazy and said he was standing on the other side all the time and there was nobody there but him. Took me a time to calm down. I know what I saw. But I never could explain it. I don't tell many people about it. But I saw that man with a light. I did.

In haunting traditions, the person seeing an apparition is often loath to discuss it. After all, it must have been bad mutton or whiskey, as Ebenezer Scrooge pointed out to the ghost of Marley: "You may be an undigested bit of beef, a blot of mustard, a crumb of cheese, a fragment of an underdone potato. There's more of gravy than of grave about you, whatever you are!" But whatever folks have seen, there is another Rocheport story that is just as strange. It happened just once, but once was apparently enough for this Columbia woman, who told her story in a 2005 interview.

I was walking the Katy Trail with a friend on a fall afternoon, maybe 2005. It was getting on towards dusk, a gorgeous day, and since it was midweek, there weren't many people out there, but every now and then a bicycle went by. We stopped to look at the river and the leaves. It was a beautiful autumn, and the trees were gold and red. The river was quiet. No barges or boats, not even any birds overhead. We were maybe a fifteen-minute walk from the station when I heard a steam whistle, which I thought was coming from the other side of Rocheport. First, I thought it was a boat, because one time I saw a steamboat replica heading upriver to Iowa, I think. I saw when the Lewis and Clark reenactors brought a keelboat upriver. So I was used to seeing odd things. But the whistle got louder, and I realized it was really a steam whistle. My friend couldn't hear it and said I heard traffic on the interstate. I stood there figuring I'd see some kids with those wooden toys, and thought they sounded really loud, but the sound kept getting closer and there wasn't anyone on the trail. Then I thought maybe I was hearing an emergency alert I didn't know. I stopped and waited, while my friend went ahead. And if the whistle blowing wasn't weird enough, I heard a train. Not quite as loud as the whistle, but I grew up near a railroad station and I know train sounds. I heard wheels, and that rushing noise and the whistle, for maybe three seconds. Then it stopped. Nothing. Like it hadn't happened. A couple were walking towards me, and I asked if they had heard the train. The man told me no and there hadn't been any trains through there in years. They kept walking, and so did I. I caught up with my friend and told her the story. I heard a steam engine and whistle that weren't there. I did not hear a train horn. But I know what I heard. I wasn't scared, but I don't like to walk in that area of the trail by myself. It was just too strange.

CIVIL WAR HAUNTINGS

No war is without its hauntings, and few conflicts have left behind as many hauntings as the Civil War. From Gettysburg to Wilson's Creek, ghosts of soldiers stalk the battlefields day and night. Some of these battlefield hauntings are aural, with the sounds of shouts and gunfire hanging in the air even as the surrounding countryside lies quietly under the sun. Other ghosts repeat their lives and deaths, caught in an ever-turning loop of sorrow.

GUERRILLAS RIDE AGAIN

Route J heads east into farm country, a winding road that now has mini-ranches and mega-homes on what used to be prairie and quiet farmland. Several miles off Route 40, just beyond Woodlandville, on the left, is a sign placed along a farm fence. It marks the skirmish at Goslin's Lane (also Gosline's, or sometimes Gosling's, Lane), which occurred in 1864, when a guerrilla attack on a Federal wagon train resulted in the usual death and mayhem. Here is the description of the skirmish from *The History of Boone County*:

> *On Friday, September 23, 1864, a Federal train of fourteen wagons, four government wagons, and the remainder pressed for the occasion, started from Sturgeon to Rocheport. The train was escorted by about seventy men . . .*

> *under Capt. McFadden. The wagons were loaded principally with some subsistence, with ammunition, clothing and private property belonging to officers and soldiers.... The escort and train travelling south from Sturgeon stopped near sunset in the lane of Sylvester F. Gosline . . . about seven miles from Rocheport. A few of the soldiers were in Mr. Gosline's yard and some of them in his orchard gathering apples. . . . On the west side of the house . . . and running north and south, there is a narrow neighborhood lane communicating with the main lane in front and southwest of Gosline's house. Without the least warning or expectation of their presence, and very suddenly, a force numbering about 100 mounted men under Thomas and George Todd and John Thrailkill charged at full speed down this lane, yelling like Indians as they came, and made a desperate attack upon the escort and train, firing indiscriminately and with deadly effect upon the soldiers. The charge was so sudden that the Federal soldiers had not even time to form in line for battle. Under these circumstances they were scattered and no alternative left but to save themselves by flight. . . . The train was taken possession of by the guerrillas. Among other things they got eighteen thousand rounds of ammunition, a lot of clothing, and private baggage belonging to the officers and soldiers. After the train had been robbed of everything the bushwhackers could use, the wagons and their remaining contents were burned. Eleven Federal soldiers were found dead on the ground and three negroes. . . . After robbing and firing the wagon train and killing and scattering the escort, the guerillas* [sic] *left the scene by the same lane through which they approached it, none of them having been killed, and only one mortally wounded. Bill Anderson was not among them.*

Another description, from *Noted Guerrillas: Or, the Warfare of the Border* by John Edwards, provides a Confederate's view of the massacre:

> *Day dawned on the 19th, cold and raw. At intervals an east wind brought rain in torrents. Nevertheless, it was to be a day of murder. Todd moved camp only a few miles, when the muddy roads and the inhospitable weather drove him into it again. Lieutenant Shepherd, taking with him Kinney, Andy McGuire, Harrison Trow, Lafe Privin, Jesse and Frank James, went scouting along the Sturgeon road until one hundred and fifty Federals were met: seventy-five infantry and seventy-five cavalry escorting seventeen wagons. The column was approaching Rocheport, with forty cavalry in advance, the infantry divided up among the wagons, and in the rear the balance of the horsemen. It was probable that one of Todd's charges would*

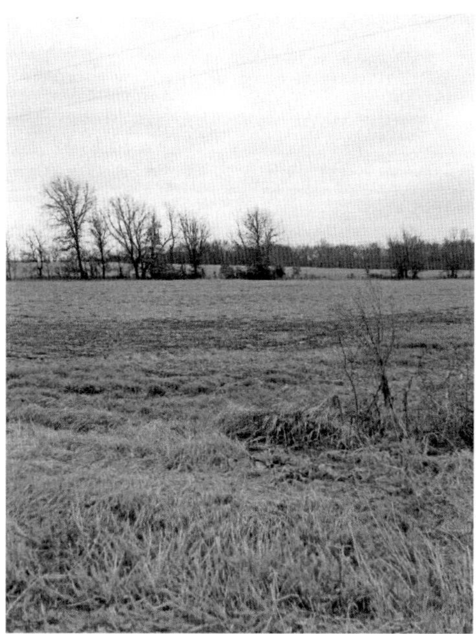
The field where the Battle of Goslin's Lane began.

make of the march a massacre. He was four miles to the left of the enemy's line of travel when Jesse James carried to him swiftly the news of the situation, but by the rapid movement of half an hour he threw himself across the main road and dashed at the cavalry in front with the old yell and the old result. Todd killed the first Federal in the fight, a handsome young captain well ahead of his men and striving to hold them for a grapple. Then the on-going tide inundated everything. Those first to the wagons, after breaking through the covering cavalry as though it had been tissue paper notched across a race-course, were Todd, raging like a lion, Thrailkill, the two Jameses, Gordon, McGuire, Hulse, Oil Shepherd, William and Hugh Archie, Mead, Kinney, Tom Todd, Privin, Glasscock, De Hart, and Vaughn. Death came to men so quickly there that something superhuman seemed to be inflicting it. Corduroyed with corpses, the muddy road in a measure became firm. . . . Past the remains . . . dashed the two Jameses, De Hart, Kinney, Hulse, Mead, and Vaughn, Jesse James killing as he galloped a Federal lieutenant two hundred yards from the road. This shot was a most remarkable one, and for some time was the talk of the command. . . . The rout, if, indeed, it were not better called a butchery, lasted until dark. Ninety-two cavalry and infantry had been killed. All the wagons were burnt, together with fifty-four Ballard rifles, abandoned by the enemy in their frantic efforts to escape. . . . The wagons were loaded with ammunition and clothing, and Todd, ordering each of his fifty-three men to help himself to a suit, the line looked as blue after the metamorphosis as any Federal line in Missouri.

Regardless of who tells the tale, the skirmish was a massacre, leaving many men dead, scores of mules killed and the Confederates in possession of Union clothing, which they would later use to advantage at the Battle of Fayette. The guerrillas met with Bill Anderson that night in the Perche Hills between Boone and Howard Counties. The following story was told by a man who lived in Harrisburg and traveled Route J daily. A more sober person did not exist, but his experience unnerved him enough to change his driving habits until his death several years ago.

> *I always enjoyed that road, out in the country then and nobody around except when they were working the fields. Thing is, the road twists pretty badly and you can be up on one rise and hear a truck coming and not know what direction it's in. So you got to pay attention. I was just heading up where J curves* [a historical marker stands there today], *when something kind of sparked over in the field on my right. I slowed to a stop and got out of the truck. It was really still, nothing moving. I couldn't hear anything from the house across the road, and there weren't any dogs or nothing to cause a noise. But I heard horses neighing and then I heard gunshots. Crack. Crack. I waited to see someone come out of the woody brush, figuring it was some hunters and wondering why they were riding horses. But I couldn't see anything moving. Then I heard yelling, kind of at a distance, but I could tell it was a bunch of men. It was strange; first I heard it in front near the woods, then across the road in back of me and to the side. It was loud enough for me to hear there were different voices, but I couldn't tell the words. Just yelling and calling and every now and then a gunshot and a neighing horse. It got worse, though, when I heard horses galloping up the road and past me. Then it stopped and was dead quiet. This couldn't have taken more than two or three minutes, from the time I got out up until the noises ended. I couldn't get back in the truck fast enough. I waited to see if anyone came by, and then I drove around to see if there were horses in a field. Nothing. And it was years before I heard anything about a battle around there. With Bloody Bill's men. It hit me then. I know as I'm standing here that's who I heard. And it will be a cold day in hell before I stop near that field again.*

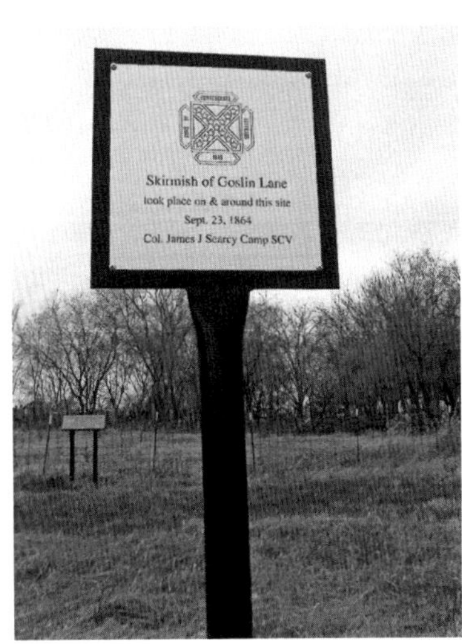

Marker at Goslin's Lane. A detailed description maker can be seen near the fence line.

House Haunted

Ghosts run the gamut in size, shape and activities, from the hazy appearances of a bouncing light to a mere shadow. And they seem to prefer houses. One 1827 Missouri account involved an abandoned cabin that was built by a husband and wife who later took in a relative suffering from ill health. But the couple grew weary of caregiving and left the man alone while they traveled. When they returned, he had died of cold and hunger, and his ghost was said to haunt the cabin, which travelers avoided regardless of weather or exhaustion. Other haunted houses are not quite as dramatic, although the following ghosts seem to have been strongly attached to their homes.

Make New Friends

Sometimes ghosts have a sense of humor. Or a sense of fairness. In the 1970s, there was a small historic house in a town outside of Columbia that was infrequently open for tours. The furnishings, including a silver service, had been left intact by the family of the widow who deeded the house to the local historical society. But the house, which was reputed to be haunted by the widow herself, had no alarms or even good locks. Local kids knew they could climb through the window and then hang out, drinking beer and talking about life, love and baseball. Once the house was closed for the season, the intrusions became more frequent, and by then the intruders didn't even have to worry about picking up after themselves. The place was a mess, and the kids didn't care. But someone clearly did, and she was not pleased.

It was a Saturday night when one club member proposed taking a silver teapot and hocking it for drinking money. The group refused and were leaving the house in a hurry when suddenly there were lights and sirens. The police had arrived and arrested everyone for trespassing. The daughter of one miscreant described what came next.

> *My dad was taken outside, and the other kids were joking because trespassing was a misdemeanor. They'd get a talking-to from their parents or get grounded for a week, but nothing more. As the police were talking to my dad, one of the officers asked if they could search his car. My dad said, "Sure," since he didn't have anything to hide, except bad judgment. But he nearly fell over when the police officer came back to the car with the silver teapot. He was terrified. To this day, he swears they did not steal the teapot and he had no idea how it got to the car, since none of the kids left the group and the doors were locked. But even stranger? The police didn't know who reported the break-in. It was a woman, but she wouldn't leave her name and she said she could see the boys sitting in the kitchen with the silver teapot. Except, you couldn't see the house from the road, there were no windows on the back of the house, the electricity was turned off and no one ever borrowed the car keys from Dad. He figured they insulted the ghost and her home, and he never did anything that stupid again.*

THE HADEN HOUSE HAUNTING

Joel Harris Haden was born in 1811 in Scott, Kentucky, and died in 1888 at his Boone County home. Haden moved to Columbia with his wife, Sarah Cave Talbott, in 1828 and took a job as a rail-splitter to help pay the bills. The couple had a daughter and settled into Columbia's society, but in May 1835, Sarah died in a typhoid epidemic, leaving behind a grieving husband and child. She was buried in the Columbia Cemetery. After Sarah's death, Haden remarried two more times, to Zerelda Kirtley and Sarah Kirtley, sisters and distant relations of his. Haden eventually owned a substantial number of slaves and established a successful farm, which grew to more than

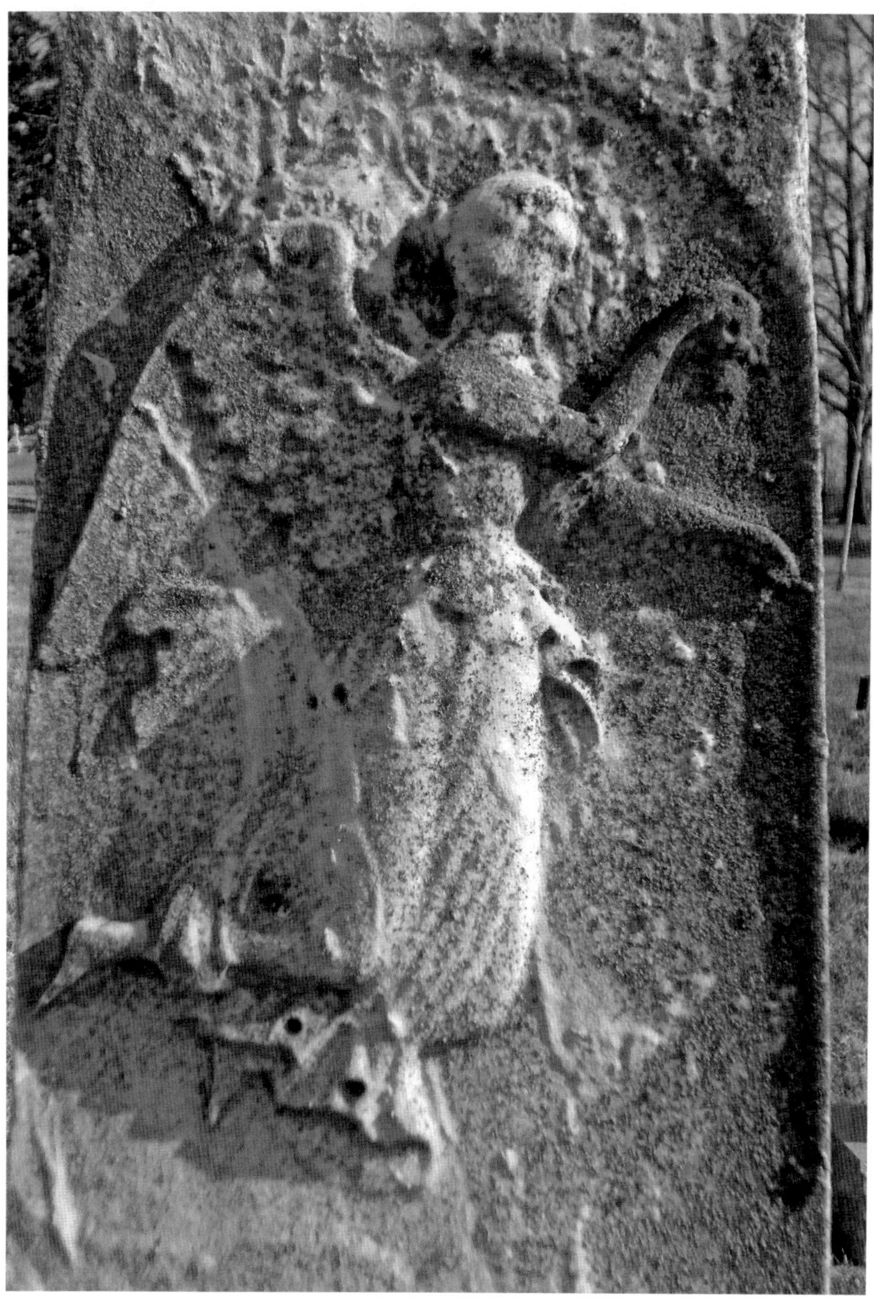

An angel happily skipping to heaven. She appears to be holding a flower, indicating a soul plucked from life.

nine hundred acres, crowned by a plantation home located on the northern outskirts of Columbia. In addition to his farming, Haden was a banker, a supporter of the new university and, later, owner of the Haden Opera House. Despite his slave-owning history, Haden supported the Union during the Civil War. His plantation home underwent several expansions, burning down in 1900. But it was later rebuilt along its original lines. The Haden House remained in the family until 1954 and later served as a restaurant and, in its declining years, a bar. Always a lively place, the Haden House apparently had visitors who popped in now and again from a different plane.

One family who lived in the Haden House in the 1970s and ran the restaurant reported their experiences with the hauntings. According to a *Columbia Tribune* interview, Haden residents saw furniture move on its own, crockery thrown across the room (to land safely and softly in one piece), objects transported from one place to another and doors rattling and shaking without provocation. On several occasions, a shadowy figure was seen drifting through the downstairs rooms, only to evaporate into dust within an eyeblink or disappear through a door. It would then appear somewhere else in the house. The modern family believed that the Haden family had remained attached to their home and were making certain that things were being cared for according to their high standards. Some people named the ghost Sarah, but which Sarah Haden was it? One Haden House inhabitant reported waking to find a young woman standing at the foot of his bed. After a few seconds of silent contemplation, the ghost faded away. Another witness told a *Vox* magazine reporter that the young woman he saw wore a long gown and had brown hair. The witness watched "Sarah" walk down the hall, and he followed her, only to see her turn down a passage and disappear. Whether or not she was aware that the living shared her beloved home is unknown, but Sarah was more startling than frightening. Unfortunately, once the home was sold and turned into a bar with a reputation for violence and drug use, the hauntings ceased. Even the most patient spirits must be appalled by earthly behaviors and move on.

Roads

Dark Hollow

Granted, this story is not set in Columbia. But for anyone who likes to take a Sunday drive, this might be one destination to avoid. It's easy to see why Route 409 near Fulton, Missouri, is known as Dark Hollow Road. Take Mokane Road south to Tennyson Road east and then, finally, County Route 409 south again, and you can find the road. It moves up hollows and through fields for several miles, ending at Ham's Prairie. The road crosses Young's Creek and then goes through an area aptly named the Devil's Backbone, which is a narrows formed between Young's and Stinson Creeks. The geography is rugged and the area is off the beaten track and isolated, despite the city being only a few miles back.

The legend tells of a large black cat that stalks hikers. The cat was freed as a result of a circus train crash in the early part of the twentieth century. While records show that there were accidents involving escaped animals, the nearest one to Fulton occurred in Centralia in 1892, with an earlier one in St. Louis in 1887. Whether or not the ghosts of any animals have made their way to Fulton is unknown, but locals have reported hearing the screeching of a big cat at night and seeing a large animal skulking through the woods along the ridges. Other local stories include a figure much like La Llorona, the weeping woman who is seeking her lost child, with witnesses hearing heart-rending screams and cries. She has been heard near a small steel bridge. Also along this haunted road is a small cemetery where people report

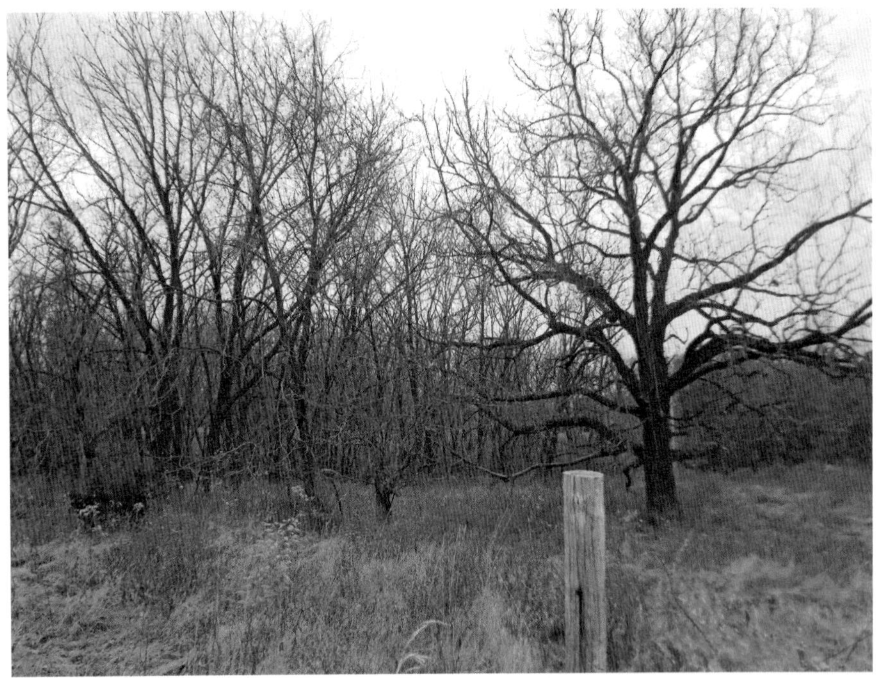

Rocheport road outside of town, where ghostly figures were seen walking in the fog.

hearing someone following them and gravestones that glow. Whether this is all legend-tripping fodder or an actual haunting is difficult to determine; the stories appear to go back a half century or so. Still, few people would want to be stranded along Dark Hollow Road after the sun sets. After all, there is that shadow.

GHOSTS ON THE ROAD

Two young Columbia men had an experience in August 1916 that made the local papers. The men were returning to Columbia when their "tin lizzie," as the newspaper called the car, sputtered to a halt three miles from town on "a night still as death save the throbbing beat of the struggling Ford." Ahead in the road, the men saw a white object floating above the ground. One of the occupants got out of the car and advanced up the pitch-black road, watching as the spirit moved silently ahead of him. It suddenly stopped and turned to pursue the unsuspecting man, who returned to the car in record time. Fortunately, "lizzie" sprang to life, and the men made it back to town safely, where their story attracted ghost hunters to the road over several nights. The spirit was not seen again, although one man claimed that it was his dogs that were out hunting that night. But the real question remains: Who was hunting who?

Another story tells how a ghost put a great racehorse on the road to success. David Judy was returning to town in July 1911 on Castor, his horse. The man and his horse were passing by a graveyard when Judy spied a ghost creep up behind them. He convinced Castor to move a bit faster—so fast that they outran the ghost every step of the way until they arrived home. Once there, Judy turned to do battle with the spirit and discovered that Castor was trailing a bolt of flannel behind him. The fabric had been attached to the saddle and unwound into the breeze, where it terrified both horse and rider. However, Castor's speed was so astounding that Judy raced the horse the next season and established a champion line whose descendants still gallop around Missouri today.

RAH, BOO, RAH, MIZZOU!

The University of Missouri was founded in 1839. As the first public university in the Louisiana Purchase territory, "Mizzou" is also the oldest public university west of the Mississippi River. Although the school has expanded through the years, the campus's heart is the Quad, where red brick and stone Ionic columns hold onto the past while greeting the future. Students still gather there for celebrations, contemplation, protests and maybe a nap on a warm day. The limestone columns that stand in the center of the Quad were quarried along Hinkson Creek in the 1840s and are all that remain of Academic Hall, which burned down in a spectacular 1892 fire caused by a light bulb. The building's janitor offered the following account in the student publication *The Savitar* in 1895:

> *I got the machine* [generator] *started up pretty well when all at once I noticed the lights go down, then go up, and about that time Boulton Clark, the fireman, said, "The building is on fire." Feeling sure that the fire was among the wires, I turned the lights off, and went to see where the trouble was. We used that night a 400-light machine manufactured by the Addison Electric Company, and so far as I can learn, we had never had four hundred lights turned on all at once before.*

The building was a total loss, but the columns remained; today, they are the symbol of Mizzou.

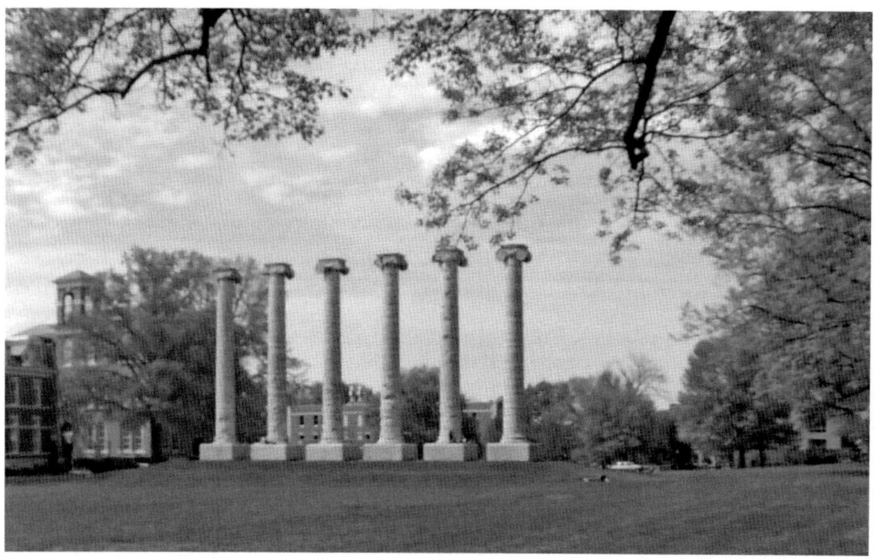

Legend says the Columns at the University of Missouri were the site of a duel and were stained with the blood of the loser.

The Columns are still associated with an unusual haunting or, better yet, a curse. According to *The History of Boone County, Missouri*, William Wedderburn Thornton and Benjamin Franklin Handy had been friends and fellow students in 1853. During a card game in Thornton's room, Thornton accused Handy of cheating. The men lived at the same rooming house, and the feud grew, as Handy insulted Thornton at breakfast. The men came to blows, and Thornton was suspended from the university for several weeks. In the meantime, Handy purchased a bowie knife and flourished a cane, telling people he would whip Thornton. A friend was asked to mediate the feud, and Handy agreed to end the argument. But on December 19, 1853, as Thornton and Handy were leaving class, Handy attacked Thornton, pinning him between an Academic Hall door and wall. Thornton managed to pull his pistol and fire at his assailant, killing him instantly. After the fight, Handy was found to have a pistol and knife on him. Thornton was later acquitted of the killing. Ghosts come in many forms: school lore insisted that the bloodstains from this duel could never be washed from the stone and that ivy no longer grows on the Columns stained with blood. Around the same time, Professor Robert Grant shot student George Clarkson in self-defense after Clarkson attacked Grant over an unrelated argument. Clarkson was mortally wounded and died a few days later. Grant was acquitted and left the university and state behind. Perhaps these deaths are tied to another odd occurrence on the Quad. In the 1970s, students reported seeing misty figures take shape there and then move through the town, ending at the Columbia Cemetery.

The Chancellor's Residence, as it is now known, is located just off the Quad. It has served as home to university presidents, chancellors and their families since 1867. Although the Residence is now the oldest campus building standing, there was a still earlier house built on the site in 1843. During the Civil War, hundreds of Union troops bivouacked on the campus, and the commanding officer lived in the original Residence. Judge Richard Gentry, in a 1913 article for an education journal, told the following story set in August 1862:

> *Two hundred confederate soldiers dashed into Columbia at about two p.m., and stationed guards at the crossings of Broadway and 6th, 7th, 8th, 9th and 10th streets, while most of the soldiers visited the county jail to release prisoners. The federal soldiers were completely taken by surprise. After the battle was over, the federal commander (Col. Lewis Merrill) was very angry and said that some Columbia citizens had informed the enemy that no sentinels or pickets were on duty (which probably was true), and he intended to retaliate by burning the town and the university building. Several union men of Columbia tried to dissuade him from such an unwise course, but he said he had determined to do so, and would do so at once. Then Mr. Robert L. Todd went to see him, and after talking pleasantly for a few minutes, with no success, Mr. Todd said, "Well, sir, you are to blame for this whole business; you should have had guards out on every road leading into Columbia, and most every other military man in the country would have done so. You have other duties besides speaking on the occasion of a flag presentation. Now, sir, if you set fire to and burn our town and our university, the friends of our town and of our university will kindle a fire under you, and I tremble for you at the result." This ended all talk about burning the town or the university. As a result of the occupancy of the university ground and building by federal soldiers, the building was damaged in various ways; and many years after that congress appropriated Five thousand dollars to pay for such damages. This money was accepted by the university authorities, and the same was used to pay for the erection of the stone entrance to the campus at the South end of eighth street.*